CW00811863

Teaching Office Skills

Teaching Office Skills

B. W. CANNING
BA, FRSA

Pitman Publishing

First published 1976

SIR ISAAC PITMAN AND SONS LTD
Pitman House, Parker Street, Kingsway, London WC2B 5PB
PO Box 46038, Banda Street, Nairobi, Kenya

PITMAN PUBLISHING PTY LTD
Pitman House, 158 Bouverie Street, Carlton,
Victoria 3053, Australia

PITMAN PUBLISHING CORPORATION
6 East 43 Street, New York, NY 10017, USA

SIR ISAAC PITMAN (CANADA) LTD
495 Wellington Street West, Toronto 135, Canada

THE COPP CLARK PUBLISHING COMPANY
517 Wellington Street West, Toronto 135, Canada

© B. W. Canning 1976

ISBN 0 273 00107 8

Text set in 11/11½ pt. Photon Imprint, printed by photolithography and bound in Great Britain at The Pitman Press, Bath

(001: 43)

Preface

This book is a continuation and extension of the work of Grace McNicol. Her book, *Teaching Shorthand and Typewriting*, was first published in 1964, and earned a well-deserved reputation among teachers and intending teachers for its combination of the scholarly with the practical, and for the wisdom of its judgements and the comprehensiveness of its subject matter. It derived these qualities from wide reading, years of classroom and practical experience, and from the dedication and enthusiasm of its author. I had the privilege of Grace McNicol's friendship for many years from which I gained greatly since she was not only a brilliant (and modest) teacher but a great person.

In this work I have tried to build further on those foundations, to extend the coverage of the book to include a separate consideration of each of the four basic office skills (shorthand, typewriting, audio-typing and transcription), to bring it up-to-date, and to embody new and forward-looking ideas about this vital but still often neglected area of education.

The book takes note of all the latest changes in syllabuses, both of students' and of teachers' examinations, and of recent developments in the provision of training for office-skills teachers.

It aims to provide a comprehensive survey of the application of psychological study and research and of ways of effectively teaching these subjects. It is my hope that wherever the office skills are taught in the English-speaking world, teachers may find it of value in their daily work and that it may prompt them to think more deeply about the nature and the aims of that work and the attainments that ought to arise from it.

For such merit as it may have, it owes much to educationists in this field in all parts of the world whom it has been my good fortune to meet and learn from. Among so many, I owe special debts to Leonard West, Emily D. Smith, Edgar Baker, Rewa Begg, Herbert Harris, Marion Angus, Dr Lessenberry, Sam Wanous, Douglas Eames, Laurie Green, Elma Whittle, Jim Crawford and to my colleagues and friends in the Pitman Group, in the Training Colleges, in the Department of Education & Science, and in the Royal Society of Arts. Certainly I have derived much from my students. I can do no better than quote Grace McNicol's own words: 'I would also like to express my appreciation to all those students with whom I have worked and from whom I have learned so much. It is indeed they who have made this book possible for in seeing them at work learning the subjects or how to teach them, I have been stimulated to clarify my own thoughts, to assess my own methods and to maintain my own enthusiasm for the subjects and for teaching.'

Though we still know too little, we go on learning about how we learn. This book is one small step along that road.

London 1976   B. W. CANNING

Contents

Preface   v
1   Learning   1
2   General Analysis of Skills Learning   6
3   Acquiring the Skills   12
4   Further Aspects of Skills Teaching   31
5   Teaching Typewriting   49
6   Teaching Shorthand   81
7   Teaching Audio-Typing   112
8   Teaching Transcription   125
9   Marking   148
10   Curriculum, Course, Syllabus and Lesson   154
11   Testing and Assessing Student Attainment   171
12   Teaching Qualifications and Teacher Training   186
Appendix: Most Commonly Mis-spelled words   195

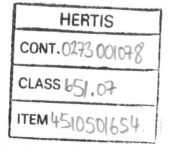

1 Learning

This book is, according to its title, about teaching. In fact, of course, it must necessarily be very largely about learning, but it is written with the teacher always in mind. The most important aspect of good teaching lies in discovering and applying the best ways of learning. Only a few decades ago the efforts of scholars and researchers were directed towards constructing, through the scientific experimental approach, theories of learning that would cover all examples of its operation. There was then a confidence in the work of scholars like Clarke Hall and Lewis M. Terman, and J. B. Watson, the behaviourist, that such a theory might be created and that we were near to discovering all the secrets of learning.

Now, in the mid-seventies, it is realized that there is no one kind of learning and that the range is such that we cannot include it all in a single category. After all, 'learning' as a word is used in a very loose way; it is not easy to define in a usable and practical form that researchers can use. As near as we can approach it at the moment (but still realized as imperfect) is such a definition as 'Learning is a relatively permanent change in behaviour that comes from reinforced practice' (*Encyclopaedia Britannica*, 1974). Reinforcement is today accepted as playing a vital role in the learning process, and may be defined as any condition that exists to promote learning, and may include such conditions as sexual stimuli or the direct stimulation of the brain cells. In the classroom, reinforcement is commonly seen in immediate knowledge of the results of learning efforts that encourage the student to continue. Ten marks out of ten, the judicious word of encouragement or praise, or an extra £5 a week, are all instances of reinforcement that work.

We have come to realize that the more we find out about learning, the more there is still to find out. 'Hills peep o'er hills, and Alps on Alps arise.'

The importance of research into learning is self-evident, but perhaps for that very reason needs emphasizing. If we can find quicker ways to learn more lastingly, the contribution to the improvement of the human condition is inestimable. To this we have to add the proviso that learning does not necessarily equate with improvement.

It was Professor B. F. Skinner and his associates who first rejected theory in favour of direct efforts to produce better learning results—for example, programmed learning.

The work of more recent researchers like D. P. Ausubel (*Theories of Learning*, 1960), Robert M. Gagné (*Conditions of Learning*, 1965) and Lee Cronbach (*Educational Psychology*, 1962) distinguishes a number of different types of learning, and it is worth starting out by giving some brief consideration to these. For a more extended treatment the books themselves should be consulted.

1 Conditioning

The remarkable, and now classic, experiments of Pavlov in this line are well known. The essence of his work lay in substituting for a simple stimulus, like the appearance of food producing the response of salivation, a second unconnected stimulus like the ringing of a bell. In the main it may be said that simple conditioning is appropriate for reactions that are mediated by the nervous system. In its most elementary form we learn from signals, like the words 'Attention, please!' in an airport, or the changing of a traffic light.

More refined instrumental (operant) conditioning in which actions are accompanied by reward or 'punishment' requires, if it is to work in normal learning conditions, a precise response to an exact stimulus. To achieve this the learning conditions need to be right, and the process (as in learning to type) is one of gradualness through an increasing refinement of discrimination. Most skills show this kind of learning.

2 Chaining

Stimulus–response situations may be linked one to another to produce a series in a definite sequence. The chaining can be both motor and verbal, and can relate, for example, to the series needed in tying a shoelace or operating a washing machine, or in learning to recite a Shakespeare sonnet.

3 Verbal association

A foreign language offers good examples of this very common kind of association learning. We learn to associate 'Spain' with 'Espana' and, at the same time, the backward association of 'Espana' with 'Spain'. In one sense we are still thinking here of learning by chaining but, because of the unique versatility of the human mind, verbal association has some unique characteristics that make it different, at least in the conditions of learning that are required.

4 Multiple discrimination

Learning is, as we know too well from experience, weakened or even obliterated over time. In discrimination learning we pick the stimulus to which we need to respond. A good example of multiple discrimination is the extraordinary learning of a lad of thirteen I know who can tell at a glance the correct name and type, together with other characteristics, of any aircraft he sees, often when far off in the sky. This kind of learning takes time because the items are very similar; the differences in the stimuli have to be most exactly noted to establish the link. But the very fact of close similarity produces interference: we 'forget' one that we have 'learned' because of another that we are learning. However, means exist to create good conditions for this necessary kind of learning which operate over a wide field—colours, shapes, letters, words, numerals, symbols and almost all distinction-learning activities.

5 Concept learning

Briefly, we can describe this kind of learning as an abstraction from all objects or happenings in a particular logical class. A characteristic of our minds is to structure our environment inwardly and give it an organiza-tion. It is this particular kind of learning that enables us to see, for example, the abstract basic when we look at a hundred solid geometric objects of any size, colour or substance, even in two-dimensional representation, and yet be able to isolate the concept of a cube from all of these and identify *only* the cubes. Quick learning comes through percep-tual organization. Kohler cites the famous example of the caged chim-panzee who had two sticks, neither of which was long enough to reach a banana, but when slotted together enabled the chimpanzee to gain possession of it.

'Thick wall it tea of myrrh seize knots trained' would be difficult to learn, until you organized perceptually its resemblance to 'The quality of mercy is not strained'.

It is in this area that the old associationists part company with the modern researchers who began to see that some kinds of learning resist associationist interpretation. In linguistics, for example, where the name of Noah Chomsky stands pre-eminent, there are some scholars who accept that a genetically-inherited concept of structure is necessary to explain the ability of a speaker or a listener to utter or understand any one out of the almost infinite abundance of possible sentences.

6 Principle learning

We acquire ideas to enable us to understand the particular from the general. A principle like 'a plural subject requires a plural verb' or 'SHUN is always on the right-hand side of simple T, D, CH or J' is grasped and we then have to *apply* it to any number of instances. The learning is really that of a chain of concepts.

Some people say that principles should be 'discovered' from instances, that inductive teaching is the best. Modern investigation suggests that there is no evidence that in fact the method achieves more thorough or lasting learning; it may spark more interest with bright students, but it certainly takes longer.

7 Problem-solving

Briefly we may say that this vital part of learning at the upper level requires the learner to devise a new principle by combining previously learned ones (Euclid was very good at it!), and thus arriving at that change in capability which is, by definition, learning.

It may also be helpful to regard all learning as having the three aspects of cognitive, affective and psycho-motor. The cognitive is all that area that embraces association through stimulus-response, which involves the structuring and ordering of learning through concepts; the affective is the area of learning in which values, attitudes, emotions and 'feeling-tone' enter—a much wider area than appears superficially; the psycho-motor is the learning that requires co-ordination of mind and physical action through sensory stimuli, operating through chains of association. Clearly, much of the learning we are considering in this book comes under the third heading, but the point to be made is that cognitive and affective aspects play a large part also and may not be ignored.

General theories of learning and the conditions under which it takes place most effectively and economically form a study that is clearly vital for any teacher. Many teachers may have acquired at least part of the ability they have by empirical means, yet there is no doubt that—as in other professions like medicine—the need for continued theoretical study and up-dating of teaching and ideas, in a period when the frontiers of human knowledge are being pushed outwards at a hitherto unprecedented rate, is essential if the standards of teaching and learning are to keep pace.

It is for this reason that I would urge on any teacher of office skills, actual or potential, experienced or probationer, professionally qualified or trainee, to take a broad view of their function as skills teachers and to continue their study of teaching and learning as a lifelong activity.

Let us conclude with a few tenets of modern learning theory that can be of particular help to us in our area of teaching and learning.

(*a*) The more meaningful the material can be made, the greater the ease of learning.

(*b*) Repetition is essential but it will become retro-active unless it is meaningful, and unless reinforcement plays a part in each repetition.

(*c*) The conditions differ for different kinds of learning but they are always crucial to its effectiveness.

(*d*) Intensive learning and practice is of special importance in the acquisition of skills. There is a limit to intensity, however, and if this is passed then intensity becomes a hindrance to and not a condition of success.

(*e*) We know that recall can be enhanced through hypnosis or actual brain stimulation. It is a reasonable assumption that other methods of increasing speed and range of recall may be disclosed which will prove to be of easier application to the usual learning situation.

Book list

Robert Gagne, *Conditions of Learning* (Holt Rinehart & Winston, 1965).
Lee Cronbach, *Educational Psychology* (Rupert Hart-Davis, 1962).
D. P. Ausubel, *Theories of Learning* (Hilgard & Bower, 1966).

2 General Analysis of Skills Learning

The subjects of study

We are setting out to study the best ways in which students may learn the four basic office skills and the most efficient methods by which they may be taught.

The four skills are shorthand, typewriting, audio-typing and transcription, and all have some features in common:

(*a*) they are all time-skills (the special nature of which we shall later explain);

(*b*) They all work through the medium of language and in particular the aural aspects of language;

(*c*) they all require the acquisition of specialized sub-skills which have to be brought up to a livelihood-earning standard.

Shorthand has a long history going back at least to 50 BC and probably before that. It was not, however, until the nineteenth century that the short symbolic representation of language, which no longer depended on the Roman letters or the quirks of English orthography, was brought to the point where it could cope with the spoken word at any speed and under almost any conditions.

It was only in the second half of the nineteenth century that it became linked to business and commerce, the law and politics. (It had been used in other applications such as drama and the Church before this.)

Fundamentally, shorthand is any method of writing that allows the individual to increase the speed of visual record of language from twice to twelve times normal handwriting speed while still retaining entire reliability in the necessary transcript.

Today, the two systems that prevail in the English-speaking world are Pitman (mostly, but not exclusively, in those areas where the historical influence of Britain and the Commonwealth has been greatest), and Gregg (in areas where the American influence has been strongest).

Typewriting is much more recent in its origins; in fact its centenary was celebrated in 1973, being 100 years from the time when Remington first produced a machine, fundamentally the work of Christopher Latham Scholes, on a commercial scale. The keyboarding of alphabetic letters has some clear advantages: it is much more legible and at least twice as fast as handwriting, and lends itself very well to reproduction. Curiously, the typewriter has remained fundamentally the same as Scholes left it, the arrangement of the characters being demonstrably very inefficient. The machine has been much refined in its mechanical aspects and appearance, and has had electricity applied to its operation, but it is in a sense an anachronism, yet indispensable and in almost universal use.

Audio-typing is of still more recent origin (about 1950) and only became possible when cheap electronic machines could be devised to record, store and retrieve the spoken word. The hopes of manufacturers that it would prove to be the panacea for the office-communications problem turned out to be illusory for a variety of reasons, some of them directly concerned with the nature of the skill of audio-typing itself. Nevertheless, audio-typing plays a complementary part in coping with the business-communications problem.

Transcription is an independent and highly important skill, the true existence of which is still only grudgingly acknowledged, if secretarial course timetables are the criterion of judgement. It is one thing to be able to write good shorthand, to be able to type, to be able to handle an audio machine, to be a good reader of manuscript—but another to combine some or all of these activities into an independent skill plus a whole range of sub-skills. The truth of this we shall see when we come to look more closely at the subject (see Chapter 8).

Characteristics of skills

All of the activities that we are studying are skills; that is to say, they require controlled physical movements to be made under the guidance of the mind, which may receive its stimulus through sensory input—as, for example, the spoken word or a sheet of handwriting—or from subjective thought, or internal prompting.

When a highly-skilled person performs a skill like potting balls at snooker, scything grass or sending a signal in Morse Code, there are always some clearly identifiable aspects of the performance. First, one is impressed by the apparent ease with which it is done, and the fluency and smoothness of the total action; if it is studied more closely one observes that everything is done in a seemingly relaxed way, and that this derives from the total economy of effort that characterizes the operation. The executant seems confident, never hesitates or pauses, and seems to carry out the action with a speed and chained integrated pattern of movements that deceive the eye.

Further study seems to show that there must be a high degree of co-ordination of eye, ear, mind and body. The actions seem to be automatic and are built-in just as a habit is built-in.

Our task is to find out how these characteristics are to be attained in our four special subjects and the best and most efficient means of arriving at this goal of accomplished performance.

Nature of skills

All the skills that we are studying are wholly or in part sensory-motor; that is to say, they usually depend upon a sensory input through the eye or the ear, or both, that occasion a sequence of trained responses which are controlled muscle contractions. It is here that the 'sixth sense' operates—the kinaesthetic sense which we all have in greater or lesser degree. This gives us the sensation of ourselves in three-dimensional space and allows us to feel, control and refine the movements that we make in the three-dimensional world. Without it, skill cannot be acquired.

A further factor in the nature of skills is the co-ordination required between mind and physical action. There is no doubt of its importance in practice, as any skill lesson with a class will quickly show, but we know too little about it. Some people seem to be blessed with a high degree of instant co-ordination and react with ease and certainty to sensory stimuli. Others—and these are the great majority—have to acquire it by means of repeated drill and practice. A few may never reach this stage and will remain permanently unco-ordinated in any skill-learning situation that demands speed of response.

The pattern of most skills, other than the simplest and most elementary, is that of a complexity of small movements welded ultimately into a coherent and integrated whole. All unnecessary actions are whittled away and the necessary ones that remain are refined to a rhythmic perfection. Economy of effort is a constant feature of all expertly-exercised skills, which must, of course, have a goal, a defined and objective purpose.

There are really four fundamental problems to be resolved:

(*a*) getting the movements right and building habits to attain this;
(*b*) grouping them into larger units of action;

(c) paring away everything needless or intrusive;
(d) aiming at the goal.

If we give these practical application in, say, typing, we have:

(i) to get the correct finger striking the correct key with the right ballistic motion;

(ii) to build patterns of chained responses (-ING -MENT -ION -ER THE AND OF TO FOR, etc). The student tackling T-H-E initially will have to approach each letter-strike as a new and separate problem. It will not be long, however, before this constantly recurring word will soon become a pattern in its own right, the fingers 'getting ready' in advance for the next movement in the chain;

(iii) to get rid of the unwanted actions—the movements of the arm and the whole hand, regressive movements, and eye movements from copy to keys to typing line to keys to copy;

(iv) the goals will define themselves as the student progresses—accuracy, evenness of impression, acceptable speed, observance of the accepted conventions and so on.

New movements require 'prompts'; in our skills we can make use of demonstration, models, verbal instructions and positive and individual guidance and help. All of these will be dealt with in more detail in Chapter 3, dealing with the efficient learning of the skills.

To get the necessary skilled movements organized into 'plans'—a coherent succession of necessary actions integrated into a chain which 'plays itself' once triggered off—we can use a series of cues that, after a time, are no longer needed. For example, when learning how to insert paper quickly and efficiently into the typewriter we can use a sequence of very brief verbal cues, such as:

Paper end-on to the left—Fingers behind paper and thumb on front—Drop paper behind cylinder—Twirl knob away from you with right hand—Lift paper release to set paper horizontal—Left and right rollers on paper margins.

and then, after some practice, the need for these dies away and we can perform the entire operation as a unit.

There is one other aspect of the particular skills that we are studying to be considered here, concerned with time. In each of the four skills a 'storage' element is necessary; between the stimulus and response there will always be an interval of time. In the case of single movements like typing 'a' or writing 'and' in shorthand it will be a very small unit of time (calculated by some researchers as between one-twentieth and one-tenth of a second). As skill progresses, the sensory input by spoken words or words to be copied from a manuscript or a shorthand note will need to be absorbed in larger groups of sounds or letters, often up to ten or more. Then the learner has to acquire the special sub-skill of acting now on stimuli that were received perhaps as long ago as 10 seconds and held in the mind for use sequentially later. This is an aspect of the nature of the skills that commonly receives scant attention.

Some skills can be performed fluently independently of any other knowledge: the typist or shorthand writer must understand the language and meaning of what she transfers to paper if she is to be fluent. A learner without an adequate grasp of language in several of its different manifestations is severely, or indeed, impossibly handicapped. The truth of this, if it needs any proof, is to be seen in the *reductio ad absurdum* of attempting to teach a symbolic phonetic shorthand to a learner who has no knowledge of the language in which the skill is to operate, or trying to teach a learner to type when the letters mean no more than Arabic script does to most of us. Other things being equal, the learner with the greatest knowledge of, and expertise in, language will invariably come out best.

Special characteristics of time-skills

There are many skills in which timing is very important but in which the sequential pace is of little consequence. One could instance ice-skating or driving a car, in which the exact moment at which to perform a movement of the total skills is very important but the length of time it takes (though it counts) is not necessarily critical to the whole operation.

In the skills under consideration, time is a vital element. How short a time the sequences of actions are to occupy is part of the goal of learning. This has the advantage that it is very easy for the student to assess his own progress and to derive satisfaction from it that will re-energize him to continue. Immediate knowledge of results (referred to again later), important in maintaining the forward drive, is constantly occurring; the learner knows both how quickly and how well he has performed.

A second special feature of time-skills is that the acquisition of the skill spreads over a fairly lengthy period. Several things result from this: firstly, there is a greater problem in maintaining the interest and the incentive fundamental to skill acquisition; secondly, much more than the customary repetitive practice is needed, and this must be made constantly meaningful if the learners are to derive greater skill attainment from it.

The pressure of time which is a continuous or, preferably from the pedagogic viewpoint, a recurring factor in learning means that the degree of co-ordination and the development of instantaneous response take on a special significance in these skills. Learners have to learn to sustain the pressures of working against the clock without a breakdown in their muscular relaxation or in their mental attitude of struggle towards success. The learner is continually in the situation of attempting to do something which, at the time, he knows is beyond him.

3 Acquiring the Skills

Conditions for successful skills learning

(a) The learner

In considering the prerequisites for success in skills acquisition we begin with the individual learner. Are there any pre-conditions that must exist before these skills can successfully be learned? Obviously there are, and in looking at these more closely we shall throw light on the ways and means by which more successful teaching can take place.

Each student is unique—a fact that in the class situation we ought never to forget. Students come in all shapes and sizes with a whole range of differing characteristics of the type fully described in basic psychological textbooks. It will help to list these differences and then consider each briefly, confining ourselves as far as we can to the actual business of acquiring the time-skills we have described. A working list of possible differences might be as follows: age, sex, physical attributes, sensory endowments, intelligence, aptitude, level of intellectual attainment, temperament and personality, interest, motivation, social sense.

Age and sex have small significance in their influence on skills acquisition. Nowadays it is usual to regard fifteen or even sixteen as the lower age limit. This does not mean that shorthand could not be taught to a twelve-year-old or typing to a seven-year-old (both have been done—often); it only means that from the cost-effective viewpoint these are the ages when the average student may learn with the best chance of success and in the shortest period. This is largely for two reasons, the first being the need for a reasonable grasp of language and the second a maturity in sensory discrimination and controlled physical movements (especially those of a delicate nature) which usually only come to a peak during late adolescence.

At the other end of the scale there is really no limit, except that physical limitations and reduced sharpness of response may begin to become apparent at any age after forty-five.

The physical attributes we have in mind are general and not specific ones. People certainly vary greatly in the degree of command they have over the muscular contractions by which the skill operates. Although much can be learned from the right drills and practice, it is still true that some students will start off with natural advantages in this respect and others with limitations which they may learn to overcome.

The fact is that a considerable part of the skills we are asking our students to acquire are delicate ones (see the very interesting analysis in the Preface to Emily D. Smith's book *High Speed Shorthand Round the World* (Pitman)) and therefore natural inbuilt co-ordination and refinement of movement are of significance. We are not at the moment well informed as to the reasons for these differences as insufficient evidence is available.

Sensory endowments are clearly a vital element: the acuity of a student's hearing, the sharpness of her sight are very important. When making the acquaintance of a new class, the teacher should discreetly assess these factors so that the right help may be given. Nor is it hearing and vision alone that are important; one reason why some people become expert tennis players or craftsmen in woodworking is the same as why others become expert typists or shorthand writers: they are blessed with a highly-developed kinaesthetic sense. It is a pity that a researched battery of tests is not readily available to assess students' capabilities in this area (see D. MacFarlane Smith, *Spatial Ability* (University of London Press)).

General intelligence as measured by IQ is also of significance as well as the more specific intelligence factors (see Hughes and Hughes, *Learning and Teaching* (Longmans), pp. 57–78). Without being too dogmatic about it, it is certainly true that if all students have IQs of 100+ their chances of success in acquiring these skills are enhanced. I should be less precise and say that, in general, students with above-average intelligence—measured on any reasonably reliable scale—will acquire office skills satisfactorily, but those of below-average intelligence will experience difficulty.

The same is also true of intellectual attainment at the time of beginning to learn the skills. In particular, a good grasp of the conventions of visual representation of the language (including spelling and punctuation), a good level of aural comprehension, of vocabulary and of the common structural patterns and idioms of the language, play a significant part in ultimate success or failure. So far as we are able to make a prognosis of success (and that is not very far), it can be said that this aspect of intellectual attainment is the most significant.

The temperament and personality of the learner are equally significant. It is in this area that the teacher plays a vital part. To bolster the will of the easily discouraged, to smooth over the ups and downs of the moody, to restrain discreetly the over-optimism and disturbing ebullience of the extrovert, to elicit more effort from the naturally indolent—these are all difficulties that the teacher can do most to resolve.

Few students are isolates; most are socially minded in the sense that they derive a tangible benefit from working towards common goals with their peers in a situation where emulation, rivalry and mutual help may, if wisely used, produce a 'plus' for each individual in the class.

Because achieving the goal of a livelihood level of attainment in these skills is not the work of a day or a week, but can be as long as two years and no shorter than four months even under the most intensive curricular conditions, sustained interest and motivation throughout the course are vital and lead us to give some special consideration to them.

(b) The learner: interest and motivation

Interest varies greatly in its origins, its nature and its intensity. When we are being entertained or amused by some witty or dramatic programme on TV, or when we are transported by some wonderful piece of music, we are interested—often to the level where our concentration is total and the rest of the external world may cease to exist for a while.

Unfortunately, the kind of interest we may hope to create in teaching skills is very unlikely to attain these levels. Out of interest comes motivation—the drive to go on that produces the effort necessary to advance step by step up the difficult slope of attainment. Luckily, interest can often be self-creating in that once a student becomes involved in the skill-learning process and is given the right instruction and the right encouragement, interest remains high and the motivating drive to succeed is maintained. This is especially true of shorthand which for some students may well become not only very interesting but often obsessive.

In this area, it is important to notice that the relationships between teacher and student are the vital ones. If a student cannot get on with a teacher, then he often does not get on with the subject; many a student's interest and progress have been lost in this way. The social atmosphere in which the learning takes place is a paramount factor; this in its turn is largely the result of what the teacher *is* as well as what he *does*. When the enthusiasm and personal involvement of the teacher are clear to each and every student then interest will flourish; enthusiasm, like measles, is catching.

Much depends also on the satisfaction the student derives from knowledge of success. This is why, if the students are to reach their goal, all the activities must be organized to produce success. Psychologists point to the need for students to have 'knowledge of results' and have them as close in time to the activity as possible. If the student is to get better he needs to know how he is progressing. However, there are some provisos to this necessary element in training for skills.

The first is that the student must understand the results; he must be able to see how successful he is in comparison with an ideally attainable result. This is one reason why the standards set must be high and, equally, why the student must know all about the activity he is being called upon to perform. Why is it being done? What result ought to follow? What time is available for it? What are exactly and precisely the expressed things that he must do? How are they best done? Only then will the student really be in a position to go for success and achieve it. The feedback will be a satisfaction out of which interest will be heightened and motivation re-charged. Even when performance has not reached a required standard it is still essential for the student to have *some* satisfaction. Without dishonesty the teacher will almost always find some aspect of performance that is better than it was and concentrate on that. Satisfaction from success is the reinforcement that will re-animate the learning process.

Having said this, it is fair to state that although interest and motivation are indispensable to learning and peculiarly important in acquiring skills, the answers to the question 'How can I create and maintain interest, and hence motivation?' are not easy ones. It is one thing to say 'You must keep the students interested' and another genuinely to accomplish it.

The subject is so central to the whole learning and teaching process that it is dealt with in considerable detail in all the texts that deal with the psychology of learning. Of all the topics of educational psychology, this is the one to study in depth and to keep fresh and up-to-date.

One always hopes that our students arrive in the course to acquire the skills because they are interested and that this is what they want to do. Regrettably, this is not always true. Students may arrive who have been press-ganged by parents or others, or who are attending (especially evening classes) because they wish to be with friends or for some other reason not directly attributable to a wish to succeed as a shorthand-typist or secretary. Even such unpromising students may succeed in the end, having acquired their interest and motivation *en route*.

To turn now from a primarily theoretical to a practical consideration of the means by which interest may be sustained and hence motivation kept strong, we may give a list of practical teaching points which will contribute to these objectives:

(i) Be interested in the students and they will be interested in the subject.

(ii) Let your enthusiasm show, if it is sincere. Enthusiasm rubs off and much of the interest of the students will derive from it. If you have little enthusiasm for the skill yourself, do not teach it.

(iii) As soon as you detect a flagging of interest, change the activity or, alternatively, the whole approach. Adopt a different method.

(iv) Seize upon the interests that the students themselves reveal and make use of them.

(v) Do not expect or require a permanently high level of interest and effort throughout a whole period of instruction. Attention oscillates even when it is close and concentrated; effort—if it is hard effort—cannot be sustained for long without a recuperation period. Go for peaks of interest and effort.

(vi) Use visual and objective methods of keeping interest alive, such as: progress charts, newspaper and magazine cuttings, good work displayed, demonstration, occasionally introducing old students who are practitioners of the skills being learned, small competitions, puzzles and challenges directly related to the skills being learned and demanding their use.

(vii) Use routine because it is economical of time and is satisfying to the learner, but also use variety constantly as well. Vary the pattern of the lesson, the approach to any new learning and the kinds of practice and drill required.

(viii) Use positive directions and encouragement. Be sparing of negative guidance or of actual reproof. A pat on the back will always do more for interest and effort than a rap on the knuckles.

(ix) Whenever practicable, join the students in their practice activities. In any case, involve yourself with them in what they are doing. The aloof maestro at the desk must disappear, to be replaced by the guide, mentor and friend; be a coach as well as a teacher.

(x) Set low standards and you will get low-standard work—you are also likely to dissipate interest. Set high standards and, although you may not always get them, the students have a clear mark at which to aim. Robert Browning has something relevant to say in *The Grammarian's Funeral*. It is the experience of years of skills teaching that when the standards set are high, but clearly and exactly understood and the teaching thoroughly effective and "involved", students will clamour to learn. (And that is not exaggerated; instances can be quoted.)

(xi) Most students will benefit from knowing why. We learn by understanding, so when students enquire why *-ore -our -oar* and *-are -ear -air* words are written with second-position heavy vowels, tell them and interest will be stimulated. And if a student wants to know why such a common letter as **A** is out on a limb, to be struck by the weakest finger of the ten, tell her that too. The little bit of history will again arouse and sustain interest.

(xii) Use intermediate goals as a means of maintaining interest. Tests in the office skills can be seriously overdone, but the establishment of clear progress markers at intervals of two to four weeks will help to keep the eye fixed on an attainable and not-too-distant target and thus, by setting up short-term goals, you can nourish interest. By considering what sensible and realistic incentives you may use, you can also keep up motivation.

(c) *The ways by which the time-skills may be acquired*
One could say that at the present stage of our knowledge of learning, there is only one way to acquire a skill and that is by doing it. We have not reached the point where we can, by subliminal instruction or by some electronic means of building into the brain, and the nerve tracks that lead from it, the correct responses to stimuli, avoid this need for a great deal of doing before the goals of the skill are reached.

However, we have learned, partly from psychological research and partly from the empirical experiences of trying things out, something of how to reduce the time spent and how to produce the most efficient and lasting results.

We have learned for example:

(i) that it is a mistake to try to learn too much at once;

(ii) that too much practice at one time is inhibiting rather than helpful;

(iii) that speed in practice is initially more important than accuracy;

(iv) that how a skill activity is carried out is initially more important than what is produced;

(v) that finding out by doing is often (but not always) better than being told or learning by heart;

(vi) that repetitive practice only produces results when it is highly specific and purposeful;

(vii) that short, frequent spells of skill learning are more effective than longer, less frequent spells over a longer total period;

(viii) that the goal for most of the time should be what most of the students can successfully attain;

(ix) that 'mark time' periods are needed to consolidate, and intervals of non-activity needed for 'reminiscence' to play its part;

(x) that what works for one group may not always work for another;

(xi) that since practice is essential, it is important to identify the most effective kind;

(xii) that time-skills are acquired best when the possibilities of error are kept to a minimum and the right habits are created from the start;

(xiii) that one important goal of skill learning is to create automaticity;

(xiv) that time-skills are more effectively learned in the class group than alone.

There are fourteen points here. We will now look at the reasons for, and the implications of, these statements in turn.

(i) *Small steps* It is a mistake to try to learn too much at once. You cannot teach the whole of the halving principle in shorthand at one fell swoop and expect students then to be able to respond correctly to the aural stimulus of words which may or may not require the application of this principle. You cannot teach students all about the layout of a business letter in one lesson and then expect them to apply all these separate items of information correctly to an example. Most people learn best by taking one step or a few short steps at a time. Besides, in this way the student is much more likely to achieve success in the application of the knowledge and skill acquired, and hence reinforcement.

(ii) *Overprolonged practice* Practice is indispensable but how long to continue one particular kind is a matter for judgement. If the teacher is too demanding then weariness or antipathy or both may set in. Instead of the forward drive of motivation being sustained, it may well be replaced by a drive *not* to do any more; what the psychologists call a 'reactive inhibition' will have set in.

Signs of this attitude must be watched for; face, gesture and actions are good guides to the student's feelings about what she is doing.

Often the practice can be given a new lease of life by slight changes in the goals or the form of it, yet still achieve the end-result desired. When I was learning to receive and send Morse Code during the Second World War I personally experienced this negative drive. Before much better training methods became widespread, the Army worked on the principle that if learners could get to 12 words a minute after 30 hours of practice, the thing to do was to lengthen the practice periods and give the learners 60 hours in the same space of time and thus, it was assumed, 24 words a minute would be achieved. Naturally, the system did not work: frustration, inhibition and sheer nervous exhaustion supervened.

(iii) *Speed v. Accuracy* That speed in practice is initially more important than accuracy is well attested by research (e.g. W. H. Solley, *Effects of Verbal Instruction in the Speed and Accuracy of Motor Skills*, Business Education, 1959). The subject has long been a controversial one, and is an aspect of skill learning peculiar to time-skills. The argument, as I see it, runs thus. Our learners must be accurate if they are going to be valued for the talents they bring to office communications. Equally they need to be quick at the job since a fast, accurate worker is clearly better than a slow, accurate one. But it turns out that the two goals are not compatible: striving for speed will almost inevitably raise the error rate while concentrating exclusively on accuracy will hold down speed.

Research shows, however, that learners who are given speed training, as long as it is controlled, will in the end attain a higher efficiency over a shorter time than those who are trained to regard accuracy as the goal from the start. In other words, students who are taught to go for speed from the start will in the end be just as accurate, but a bit faster, given the same time allocation.

The reason for this may well be that in shorthand and in typewriting the execution of the movements changes its whole nature between fast and slow. The 'flick' style of shorthand writing and the swift staccato on–off action of key-striking in typewriting require subtly different muscular contractions from the slow stroke-by-stroke shorthand writing or the slow pressure on the key. In fact, learners find this important aspect of training a little hard at first, but it does not take long to get the correct response. What is needed, of course, as near as possible, is the *same* response in Lesson 1 to that necessary in Lesson 100. The difference is only one of closing the gaps—the gaps of time that elapse between the swift penning of one outline and the next, or the crisp striking of one key and the next. As the training proceeds, insistence upon accuracy increases and we must teach by switching goals from 'get it down' to 'get it right'. Only in the end-product can we attain the reconciliation of the two incompatibles, which the realistic situation of actual work demands.

Another point already mentioned is relevant here. Only by students trying to go faster can they succeed in becoming faster. As long as this situation is controlled so that the prize is not dangled too far away for the earnest student to reach by a number of small upward steps, the next intermediate goal is achieved and then consolidated.

The potential is almost always there. Few students leave comparatively short courses today at anything like the level of their real potential. This is why in-service training for specified targets almost always succeeds if the right incentives are there. Which leads us on naturally to a brief consideration of our next point:

(iv) *'How' is more important than 'what' initially* Perhaps this is truer of typewriting than of shorthand, but it applies to both. If the penmanship elements of shorthand learning do not get ample emphasis at the start—if the ballistic action of key-striking is not the main aim in learning the keyboard—wrong habits will be produced. And everyone knows that getting rid of a bad habit is even harder than acquiring a good one! So what the typing line reveals in the earlier lessons is less a matter for concern than the way in which the necessary activities are being performed.

(v) *Induction and discovery* Finding out by doing is often (but not always) better than being told or learning by heart. Certainly in the practice of the skill itself it is only doing that can be effective; nevertheless, it must be guided and channelled into the right directions if the right habits are to emerge. As to the intellectual content of both the skills of shorthand and typewriting, these will often lend themselves to the discovery (inductive) method in which a general conclusion is reached from particular examples.

Suppose, for instance, that the students know nothing of the abbreviated **W**; then we could approach the subject something like this:

Read with the students the first seven outlines (a) and elicit from them what the common feature is—viz. they all begin with the sound **W**. Then we could present (b) and say: 'Go on reading in the same way with **W** as the first sound'. Then we would ask what conclusions were to be drawn. The answer will probably come back: 'The little semi-circle stands for **W**.' 'What kind of a little semi-circle?' 'A right motion semi-circle.' 'Vertical or horizontal?' 'Vertical.' Then we would sum this up: 'So a little vertical right motion semi-circle stands for **W**. Now the question is 'When?' So step by step you would draw out the right answers, viz. when it is the first sound, and when it comes before

K G M R (up) and R (down). At that point we put up a fresh list of examples:

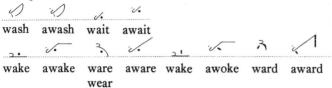

wash   awash   wait   await

wake   awake   ware   aware   wake   awoke   ward   award
                 wear

and once again proceed by reading the fully vocalized outlines without telling the students what they are, inducing them to derive a further point from what they observe, viz. that semi-circle W is used before K G M R (up) and R (down) if the W is the first sound in the word. When a vowel precedes initial R then the stroke W is used. But it would take some time to get the general rule expressed as precisely and unambiguously as that. Indeed, it would take a long time for the whole operation, usually about three or four times as long as a deductive or 'telling' approach. The argument is that, by virtue of the fact that students have struggled mentally through the process to arrive at the right conclusions, the learning will be more lasting.

Our own views, from long teaching experience on this point, are that the game is only rarely worth the candle where shorthand and typewriting are concerned. It may occasionally be used to bring variety to the lesson but it delays activity for too long; and, moreover, the best students are those who provide the thinking while the mediocre or inferior ones are those who trail along in their wake, the net result being that they are 'told' while the bright ones, who don't need it, induce.

In typewriting there are probably more opportunities of using discovery, as for example in teaching tabulation, but even here the time-consuming aspect of the 'do-and-discover' method must be carefully watched. In more academic subjects, no doubt, induction and discovery can, with advantage, play a larger part.

There is, in fact, nothing disreputable about plain 'telling'. Telling is itself an economical method of instruction which is capable of a whole range of different approaches. If, just to give one example, students are learning about tick H, it could be presented in a bald, precise statement:

'When H is the first sound in a word and is followed at once by M, L or downward R, you write a shorthand sloping tick before the M, L or downward R like this:

home   hell   here

Now read these words as I write them up . . .'

But equally I could begin by writing one or two very large downward
H's on the chalkboard or OHP transparency and then say: 'Look
what happens when I cut the top half off. I am left with this / —and that
is **H** too but only before **M, L** and downward **R** . . .' and then go on from
there. Or I could begin differently again and say: 'Look, this is
downward **H** when it stands all alone as in high, hay—or in
words that come from such single-stroke words highly,
haystack. These are words where downward **H** is used before **K** and
G— hook, Haig. Now look at these home, heel,
hair. But wait. I'm going to shorten these **H**'s like this. . .'

Besides, plain telling enables you, by varying your presentation and
the words you use, to *re*-present the same idea in two or three different
ways until it is grasped.

Again, learning by heart has its obvious place. I bless the day my
teachers obliged me to learn by heart such poems as 'Lord Ullin's
Daughter', 'The Burial of Sir John Moore' or 'Ozymandias'; formulae
and sections of fundamental arithmetic have to be learned by heart. In
the end we learn the typewriting keyboard by heart and could reproduce
it on paper from memory. Is there any place for this (rote learning) in the
skills? A modest one, I would say. Little recurring difficulties can
sometimes be avoided by knowing this vital rule by heart (one I have
always required my own students to commit to memory): 'If a third
place vowel comes between two consonants the vowel goes in the third
place before the *second* consonant' *and* 'In a third place outline it's the
first up or down stroke that goes through the line. Think of *mill* and
think of *nil*; think of *kill* and think of *gill*.'

(vi) *Meaningful repetition* Repetition is a necessary part of the process
of acquiring the skills. The danger is that it may become monotonous,
mindless and unproductive, and when this happens progress comes to a
halt and boredom begins.

There are two basic ways of avoiding this. The first is to make all
repetitive practice meaningful; the second is to introduce slight
differences into each repetition, thus demanding the mental application
that is needed to produce progress and keep interest alive. To be
meaningful, the repetition has to be completely specific and intelligible.
Before it is attempted the student has to understand exactly what it is
that has to be done, what time is available, what its aim is and how the
attainment of that aim is to be assessed, precisely how the repetition is

to be performed and what particular ideas have to be kept uppermost in the mind during its performance.

To illustrate these we can use an example from typewriting for the first, and one from shorthand for the second.

For example, the letters e and i may get confused in typing. Therefore we produce a sentence in which these predominate: 'She will receive this receipt in triplicate if she requests Philip to send it.' (80 strokes—11 e's, 11 i's.)

We tell our students that the object of the exercise is to type several correct versions, never getting an e or an i wrong. We tell them that there are 80 strokes and that we are going to have four attempts. We begin with an untimed type-through allowing the students to watch themselves make the correct key-strikes and to say out loud each e and each i as they strike it. The second one will be allowed one minute, 16 wam; the third 45 seconds, 20 wam; the fourth 30 seconds, 32 wam. Now we have created the right mind-set and answered all the questions posed in the paragraph above.

For our second illustration we use a penmanship exercise in New Era shorthand based on the initial **R** hook series. We give a 20-word sentence like this: 'For particulars of a number of price increases for trips abroad and for journeys to Greece, write to this address.'

We get a correct copy of this shorthand written on to one line of a shorthand notebook using the margin as well. Then we tell the students that the aim of this repetitive drill is to write this sentence at an exact speed from dictation, first at 60 and then at 80 wam; the hooks are to be small and round every time. Their goal is that the third or fourth repetition shall be as perfect in its accuracy as the copy that they have just prepared. Then after, say, two at 60 and two at 80 wam, occupying only about two minutes, we introduce a change, 'Greece' to 'Germany'. And after one more at 80 and one at 100, we change, say, 'trips' to 'travel' and 'address' to 'person'. In this way we keep the mind alert to *what* is being written, which is as important as *how* it is being written.

(vii) *Allocation of learning time* All experience and research show that the best results in learning the time-skills come when the periods are fairly short and frequent, the total learning time being spread over a period which varies depending on the skill being taught, but generally within 16–40 weeks.

Acquiring the skills, if the training is of the correct intensive and hard-working kind, is a tiring activity; only when they are wholly mastered and substantially automatic are we able to work at them for lengthy periods without fatigue and nervous weariness. For this reason periods of about 35–60 minutes seem to be best for average young students. The practice of 'double-headers' of $1\frac{1}{2}$–2 hours, which are often to be observed in typewriting, is not one to be recommended.

How frequently these shortish periods should recur is another problem. The experience derived over several years of courses of various lengths at Pitman seems to show that well-motivated and mature students can sustain up to three or four such periods a day with cost-effective benefit (i.e. the students will attain a higher level in a shorter total instruction time). At the other end of the scale, less than one such period of skill training each day results in far too much regression and some dissipation of interest too. There is little doubt that for the majority of people the most successful way of acquiring the time-skills is by frequent shortish periods of learning repeated often within a restricted overall period of time.

Still, there must be intervals for the psychological phenomenon of reminiscence to play its part. Learning takes place not only during the training period but between the end of one and the beginning of the next. However, it would seem that this only takes place when there is a fairly long time lapse of 12 hours or more.

Continuity is also very important. Teachers of any experience will know very well the harmful effects on learning of long holiday periods or absences. With many of our courses still linked to the ancient custom of the academic year, the intervention of holidays of any length longer than a day or two can be clearly shown to be a serious drawback to the acquisition of time-skills. Recency, as well as frequency, is highly significant in skill learning.

It is unfortunate that sometimes timetables are constructed by those who have no practical experience of skills teaching. There are difficulties: the demands of other subjects in the curriculum, of establishing the right balance of 'contact' hours, of the logistics of availability both of staff and equipment. Nevertheless, if the office skills are to be learned in the right way and to the level of livelihood-earning attainment, then a fresh look has to be taken at these problems. There is much to be said for a weighted timetable that does not give equal emphasis to all subjects of the curriculum throughout the period of a course. During the main period of skill learning, consideration should be given to a limitation of the curriculum to enable the correct frequency and intensity that is needed to be incorporated. Later, when the skills are well on the way to successful acquisition, the curriculum may then be advantageously expanded. These problems are gradually being more widely understood and steps taken to solve them.

(viii & xiv) *The class and organization for success* We have already referred to the important fact that a class of, say, twenty-five students is a group of twenty-five different individuals, each of whom will need to be understood and given individual attention and guidance.

The further important fact to be remembered is that a class develops social and communal aspects of its own; no two classes are identical. Every teacher will appreciate the fact that two classes, on the face of it having similar students of equal age, attainment, and aptitude, will for all that develop their own internal chemistry; often the class as a group may act as the catalyst for success. Being by nature gregarious, we can derive a satisfaction from working with others who, like us, share common aims; mutual help, discussion, a modest amount of emulation and competition may, if the teacher makes cautious use of these things, be very beneficial to the individual in the class. For each separate class, the teacher will need to develop slightly different attitudes and approaches, which can only be derived from a sensitivity to, and an understanding of, this class ethos.

The counter-current to this, which we have to do our best to resist, is that less successful students may become despondent and lose their interest and drive after comparing their own lack of achievement with the progress of their quicker class peers. Up to a point we can hope to remedy this by special help, encouragement and extra practice outside the normal class hours. When many students are following the same course in three or four different class groups, there is the further solution of re-grouping. Students who are slower are not necessarily failures; there are many recorded instances of those who were not at all successful initially, yet who subsequently became outstanding students. A classic instance of this is Marion Angus, originally near the bottom of the class, but now one of the world's greatest exponents of the office skills.

In skills work, nothing succeeds like success. It is therefore vital that the practices and activities which the class are called upon to do should not only (as we have shown) be precisely and exactly understood, but they should also be of a kind that the majority of students can succeed in, and in which all can attain some measure of success.

To foster this idea of working successfully in the class towards common goals, it is important also that the guidance and help given should be positive. 'Don't' calls attention to what is not wanted and gives it an emphasis; the student wishes to know 'what?' and 'how?' and not 'what not' and 'how not'. 'Don't move any part of your body for 30 seconds!' contains an in-built compulsion to move. 'Try your powers of self-control. See if you can keep every part of you quite still for a time—say 30 seconds' is an approach much more likely to succeed. Encouragement and approval of even minor improvements will lead to larger ones.

(ix) *Consolidation* In the development of the skills it is necessary, at fairly short intervals, to have a pause of perhaps one or two sessions when no attempt is made to push the skill farther, but to consolidate and reinforce what has so far been attained. This is the reason why in modern texts for the office skills, Review Units are often incorporated regularly.

In fact, progress in time skills can more realistically be seen as a series of steps rather than as a smooth curve, (*a*) rather than (*b*).

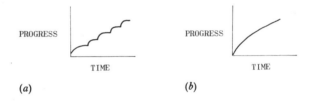

(*a*)   (*b*)

The analogy of mountain-climbing is relevant: the climbers make their way up by one bold exploratory effort, and then consolidate and make secure their position before going on to the next ascent.

When the steps elongate into platforms we have the 'plateau' situation where a skills learner, having reached a certain level of attainment, finds it exceedingly difficult to go on. In fact, the 'plateau' situation, while it exists, is less frequent than is supposed, especially when the learning/teaching conditions are right.

However, a plateau may evince itself in a time-skill for the following reasons: a falling-off in interest, reaching the supposed or actual limit of individual potential, the replacement of lower-order habits by higher-order, a changed method needed to operate the skill. I had personal experience of the last of these when I had reached 100 wam in shorthand and wished to go on to 120. For a long time I 'stuck', the reason being that I had grown too used to working close up to the dictation; but now that the words were coming faster I found it necessary to change my method and work farther away, without panicking. An illustration of the penultimate reason arises when students, who have been kept too long on typing to music or metronomic typing, have to switch to the chained digrams and trigrams of more expert typing (see Chapter 5).

(x) *Varying methods and approaches* Because of the differences in class groups already referred to, sensitive and alert teachers will be ready to change the approach and the method from knowledge of the class as a whole. A standard set of notes and examples for a whole course may be a useful standby from one year to the next, but it ought not to be regarded as a unique methodology as well. The presentation, practice, emphasis, allocation of time and types of activity chosen may all need some changes according to one's interpretation of class needs.

In these and most other matters of skill learning, the difference between knowing all the theory and all the methods on the one side, and the kind of person the teacher is on the other will be a measure of the difference between standard competence and outstanding success.

(xi) *Effective practice* Practice being an essential part of all time-skill acquisition, it is important that the most effective conditions for it should be known and acted upon all the time. These conditions may be stated as:

(1) The aim of the practice must be precise.

(2) The student must understand this aim.

(3) The aim must be appropriate to the needs and capabilities of the student.

(4) The practice period should be sufficiently long for the students to gain benefit from it, but not longer than is necessary to achieve the aim.

(5) If signs of fatigue, boredom or frustration are noticed, the practice should be stopped.

(6) Periods devoted to drills should always be of short duration, but should be regular and frequent.

(7) The physical conditions in the room (accessibility of materials, lighting, temperature, ventilation) should be as good as possible.

(8) The same goal or the same practice material (especially drills) will not always be appropriate for a whole class or group. Material and goals should be selected to help individual students.

(9) During practice the teacher should observe the technique and work habits of the students.

(10) Praise for improved technique (however slight) is more important than correction. It helps to build up the confidence of the learner—an important feature in skill acquisition. Praise is especially important with the less successful students.

(11) Students learn more effectively if the material on which they practice is meaningful to them.

(12) Purposeful material (material which will be used) is often more valuable than mere exercises, but it must be appropriate to the stage of attainment of the student and must never be out of step with the planned course.

(13) Practice must be continued to the point of 'over-learning', that is, beyond the point where the material learned can just be recalled, or the activity just accomplished but with effort (see (xiii) below).

(14) Practice must be devised so that the connections or transitions between the sub-skills are in their turn practised; otherwise the right associations for the employment of the total skill may not be created.

(xii) *Error reducing and good habit formation* Avoidance rather than correction of error must be a dominant aim in skills teaching. Errors will be made, of course; even the expert will write the odd incorrect outline or strike the wrong key on the typewriter. Anyone who first tries out any skill is bound to make numerous errors. There is no escape from this and no harm in it either, as long as it does not lead to the establishment of a wrong habit. This is why, when shorthand is being learned and before all the rules are known and understood, or the first 1,000 words have become 'stamped in' and made instinctive, it is better to restrict 'free' dictation at any speed to a very small percentage of the whole. It is also the reason why, in the keyboard stage of typewriting, that we need to place the whole emphasis on the correct striking action and the speed of it, because it is known that more than half of typewriting errors derive from faults of technique.

It is part of the teaching task to shield and protect the student from error and to create the best conditions possible for learning and practice. By doing this we allow the student to build up the right habit and 'stamp it in' in the psychological sense of over-learning. The alternative is the more painful one of eradicating the bad habit, and there are few more irksome or difficult jobs in life than that.

A natural process for most observant students is to shed their own errors one by one. In a true sense, the ultimate total skill can be seen as a process of continuous refinement. If we call too much attention to the errors the student is making, we may inhibit the development of the skill. It is a matter of judgement: clearly gross errors or imperfections of technique must be stopped at once; for the less serious defects, the best approach may well be to comment favourably on the correct elements observable in the skill and to focus the student's attention on these basics.

The best ways towards good habit formation are: encouragement of the correct elements; stopping gross errors; providing ample demonstration; providing good verbal cues; excluding the conditions under which bad habit formation may arise.

(xiii) *Automaticity* Some people jib at this term because they interpret it as mindlessness, or confuse it with the idea of turning students into automata. In fact, the development of automaticity in a sensory motor skill has an opposite effect: it liberates the higher conscious mind from the stress of the skill and allows it to pursue its proper task of thought, anticipation, problem-solving, memorizing and the application of intelligence to the overall handling of the task.

We probably all remember how stressful and arduous it was when we first set out to master the typewriter keyboard or to interpret audio bleeps as letters and words in the Morse Code. Our whole mind had to be concentrated on the task before us, and much energy and nervous force had to be used up to enable us to learn what do to—and still more—command the means of doing it.

Only when over-learning has taken place and the student's response to the word 'therefore' in typewriting is triggered off as the-re-for-e without an instant's thought, or to the words 'and we have been' in shorthand is ⌢⌣, in which the form flows on to the paper with no more thought than if she were writing her own name, is the student then confident and in command. Then she can give conscious attention to the arrangement of the words on the typing paper and to the nature of the content or, in shorthand, answer the silent questions that arise in the mind: 'where is the full stop?—a vowel is needed to help me read this word—shall I use figures here when typing from the note?—but A.J. told Mr Johnson this already in a letter he wrote last week.'

It is worth noting that the greatest skill exponents have always been ready to carry their over-learning far beyond what most people would think sufficient. I have seen a page of Emily D. Smith's notebook black with endless repetition of the same lines in order to increase still further the perfection and uniformity of outline. I have seen Thelma Chalmers, June Swann and Margaret Ball type a particular paragraph, rich in the trigrams or even quadgrams that they were aiming to chain into a single response pattern, over and over again in order to shorten just a microsecond more the gap between one letter and another.*

---

* This is a kind of typing practice only for experts and not for learners.

The goal of total automaticity is, of course, unattainable because the variation in the word patterns arising from the generative syntax of language is infinite. With our learners taking only a comparatively brief course of instruction we can only hope to automaticize a few hundred words. However, even this is a great step forward; after all, 69 words represent 50 per cent of all continuous English matter.

Therefore, it pays to regard some degree of automaticity as attainable and to work to achieve it.

4 Further Aspects of Skills Teaching

Demonstration

At all stages of skill acquisition good demonstration is an important—and often a vital—part of teaching; in acquiring a skill we learn by imitation. Probably we do not demonstrate office-skills activities as frequently as we ought, although the opportunities are numerous and should be utilized. This list is not intended to be comprehensive, but suggestive of the kinds of basic and sub-skill activities in which the student will benefit from demonstration.

Shorthand

How to write particular forms (e.g. initial hooks)
How to use the margin
How to turn the notebook page
How to build mental 'storage'
How to hold the pen
How to write with the lightest touch
How to 'flick' write
How to sit and how to position the hands
How to write at speed

Typewriting

How to strike the keys
How to operate particular important manipulative devices (e.g. shift-lock, carriage return)
How to insert paper, envelopes, cards, stencils
How to set tabulation stops
How to place copy and work from it
How to use an ink duplicator

Similar lists could easily be made for audi-typing and for transcription.

The characteristics of good demonstration are these:

(*a*) The demonstration must be expertly given. Thoughtful preliminary practice is recommended. A smooth, efficient, rapid performance will set the standard for the learner.

(*b*) The demonstration must be as brief as possible. The learners' natural desire is to imitate at once, and not too long a gap must be left between watching and doing.

(*c*) Call attention only to the salient points of the activity that are vital to success. On the whole it is true that the fewer words used, the better.

(*d*) The actions required are often fairly complex; therefore an analysis stage is needed. The learners cannot be expected to put it all together without being conscious of the constituent parts.

(*e*) Every learner must have a clear, unimpeded, right-way-round view of the demonstration.

Let us consider some of the implications of these characteristics. In shorthand, the chalkboard is a quite indispensable piece of equipment: used with skill, speed and confidence, chalkboard writing will play a continuous part in setting up models for the learner to imitate. Some teachers use lined boards to assist in position writing; to others, lines are constricting. Shorthand outlines do not need to be always the same size: if we are demonstrating, for example, initial hooks or tick **H**, a larger style than usual will help the learner to appreciate the points that have to be learned. However well the chalkboard demonstration is given, it is divorced in obvious ways from reality.

A superior means of demonstrating shorthand is the pen and notebook but, unfortunately, this limits the class to only four or five students at a time unless we are fortunate enough to be able to use CCTV. Nevertheless, it is the best way and use should be made of it from time to time even though it is time-consuming. The learner will gain much more from actually seeing the pen glide over the paper and watching the teacher's movements at close quarters than from chalkboard outlines on a vertical surface.

Here, as in typewriting, demonstration by video tape with a close-up moving picture offers a great hope for the future.

In typewriting, use is often made (and more should be made) of a demonstration stand on which the picture opposite is an illustration of an appropriate type.

The demonstration stand suffers from some obvious drawbacks of which the most important is the difficulty of ensuring that all the students have a clear view and can see well enough to appreciate the activities being demonstrated. It is more effective to have a proper typewriting surface with adjustable chair, and typewriter permanently available in a clear space so that seven or eight students at a time can get an exact idea of the activities demonstrated.

Most demonstrations fall naturally into three parts. First there is the complete demonstration commented on briefly by the demonstrator with just the salient points emphasized; this can be run through two or three times. If the activity is complex enough to warrant it, the

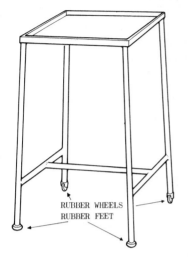

TRAY

Length: 38 cm (15 in.)

Width: 53 cm (21 in.)

Depth: 1.2 cm (0.5 in.)

STAND

Height: back 98 cm (38.5 in.)

        front 97 cm (38 in.)

Width: top 50 x 36 cm (20 x 14 in.)

        bottom 53 x 48 cm (21 x 19 in.)

RUBBER WHEELS

RUBBER FEET

demonstration is now broken down into three or four separate parts, each being illustrated separately and then finally resynthesized into a whole. The next stage is for the learners to practise what they have been shown. At this time the teacher will move among them, guiding and helping and noting the points that need to be clarified or re-emphasized. Now the learners have 'the feel of it' and are in a better position to appreciate the final stage, which is a repeat of the demonstration with verbal comments modified by what the teacher has picked up by observing the learners at practice.

It should be noted once again that opportunities for helpful demonstration occur as frequently at a fairly advanced stage as they do at the beginning, and should be used as a teaching technique.

Transfer of training

Many of the books on the subject will contain good accounts of transfer of training. In particular, pp. 209–33 of *The Psychology of Learning and Techniques of Teaching,* James M. Thyne (University of London Press) ought to be read by all office-skills teachers.

The fundamental point is this: by learning one thing you may make it easier to learn another; that is 'positive transfer'. For example, it was my experience that having reached a good level of attainment in one time-skill, shorthand, it was much easier for me than my fellow-students to acquire another, Morse-Code reading. On the other hand, learning one thing may make it measurably more difficult to learn another. For example: ' "High negative transfer from playing the banjo to playing the guitar" would mean that playing the banjo had a very bad effect on one's subsequent attempts to play the guitar' (Thyne, op. cit.).

Transfer may arise either from a similarity of content, as between say Latin and Spanish, or from a similarity of method, as between typing and piano-playing. The general conclusions from researches into transfer may be summarized as follows:

Positive transfer

1. For such transfer to take place there must be common elements usable in the two subjects or situations.

2. Students must be aware of the common elements.

3. Students must have the opportunity to use these elements in the new situation.

4. There is generally more positive transfer if the teacher makes an effort to secure it through appropriate teaching methods and material, and in particular to the similarity of cues.

Negative transfer

1. This takes place when the two subjects or situations have elements which vary only slightly, or in some but not all aspects.

2. Negative transfer takes place in motor activities when either the stimulus or response (but not both) is changed from one situation to another so that a correct habit in the one is incorrect in the other (e.g. transfer of ability on one make of typewriter to another).

Verbal instruction

Clearly words—written or spoken—are indispensable in the learning process of any activity other than the simplest. It is a not uncommon complaint about experienced teachers that they use too much 'chalk and talk'. Certainly in skills training it is all too easy to use too many words—to become a lecturer instead of a coach—and is a hazard all teachers run and has to be guarded against. It pays to be consciously economical of words in the class-learning situation; on the other hand, repetition will be necessary if the right learning, i.e. the right responses to the situation, are to take place. What then is to be done?

Verbal instruction fulfils the following functions: explanation (why? how? when?); cue for action (recipes, installation and operating instructions, performance of an activity); resolving doubts, answering questions (teacher/student two-way communication); backing demonstration, diagrams, models; formal 'telling'.

It is in the first, third and fifth of these functions that the tendency is to say too much and thus cloud instead of clear the learner's mind.

So we must be precise and exact but at the same time concise, even brief. The same thing will need repeating. Sometimes saying it again in precisely the same way will be effective but, more often, putting it into different words will be better. Actual instructions should be firm, quiet, but forceful and authoritative; explanation should be bright, colloquial, even figurative.

A language difficulty will often arise. We have to learn, as instructors, how to frame what we say in terms immediately and wholly understood by the learners. Sometimes the actual terms that have to be used will need to be explained before we can go on. A further factor of importance will be the clarity of enunciation, the audibility and the acceptability in terms of regional pronunciations and linguistic usages of the teacher's voice and speech. A Pakistani teacher, however expert, is sure to run into such difficulties when teaching in, say, Cheltenham; a London teacher in the Gorbals.

Common problems in time-skills learning

Teachers of time-skills such as shorthand and typing face a number of recurring problems. While the impact of these problems will vary from one place to another, or in one course compared with another, the office-skills teacher of even comparatively brief experience will have come up against all those detailed below.

1 *Varying level of linguistic knowledge*
How well the student is acquainted with his own language and how easily he moves in it are factors that the office-skills teacher soon realizes are vital. The would-be learner who knows no English cannot learn an office skill; one who has a good knowledge can. Going one step farther, does this mean that a learner who starts off with a complete command of the language will do best? Not necessarily—because there are other factors involved. But certainly such a learner, other things being equal, should do much better.

What are those elements in language that seem most relevant from the viewpoint of the learning of office skills? A wide recognition of vocabulary obviously helps: not every learner will recognize *proliferate* or *mordant*, but you hope they will all recognize *increase* and *biting*. If they do not, you as a teacher are in trouble right away.

Also, some familiarity with the common structures of the language and the recurring collocations of words is of great value. To give an example:

> John Williams, our .... Secretary, who is now in .... of the Society's accounts, states in his annual .... that our income from the .... of members .... more than .... over the past three ...., and that this .... from a 10 per cent .... in the number of members and a 30 .... in the annual .... subscription.

To a student knowledgeable in vocabulary and structures this sentence, full of gaps, is nevertheless, given a little thought, perfectly meaningful. It can be reconstructed with a high likelihood of accuracy.

In the same way there are many commonly occurring collocations of words, cliches very often, which we can hardly avoid using in everyday non-literary communication. It is only necessary to set down an example or two for the point to be recognized:

> *Last but ... .*
> *This went on for a very ....*
> *Present company ......*
> *We thank you for ....*
> *They went at it hammer ....*

Even if you failed to get down any note for the missing words, you would be able to supply them.

In addition, it appears clear from research done on this topic that ability in language has also to be associated with agility. The swift mental response and interpretation is as important as the knowledge itself.

In typewriting, the element of fast reading and comprehension has been shown by Lillian Malt, in her skills-analysis method of tackling the problems of keyboard operatives, to be the vital element to teach in order to secure speedy and accurate keyboarding.

Where the teacher has a group in which there are wide differences of level in language attainment, divergences in attainment in the writing skill will inevitably arise and cause greater or lesser trouble. This outcome is separately discussed below.

2 *The aural problem*

The characteristics of our overall learning system in education are such that students do not generally think much about the sounds that they hear; nor are they often given any special training in listening. The extraordinary orthography of English, with its single characters being used to represent several different sounds and its representation of the same sound appearing in several different ways, clouds the issue further for the learner.

The result is that many students find it difficult to identify sounds or to distinguish one from another. Others can give no clear distinction even between a consonant and a vowel, still less a diphthong. If asked how many separate sounds there are in words like *caw, calm, coughing*, they are unlikely to be able to say, still less to identify clearly each one. The same is true of syllabication in typewriting.

This deficiency in knowledge and understanding does not matter so much perhaps for the ordinary traffic of everyday life. When it comes to learning a new form of visual representation—then it is at once very important.

Our students for the most part have not been trained to get close enough to words either from the aural standpoint (so as to be able to distinguish ĕ from ĭ, consonant from vowel, sound from symbol) nor to see and grasp the visual differences that are so important in the typewriting activities (sharpness of literal perception, ability to locate and correct error).

The other aspect of this matter is the ability to listen and to comprehend. We teach children to read, but we only teach them incidentally to listen with understanding. Our present techniques for this kind of instruction are not well developed. Nor can it be assumed that because a student is good at the mental *reading* of a piece quickly and with understanding, he will necessarily show an equal facility in *hearing* and comprehension.

Does this matter? It certainly does for any student of skills, a large part of whose main input is going to be an aural one, and that applies to shorthand, audio-typing and transcription.

This is a field in which more research is needed. But what is apparent to anyone experienced in recording notes from aural stimulus is that if the writer does not fully and immediately understand what he hears there will be an instant fall in the level of his ability—even though the words themselves are familiar enough to him. Therefore it is worthwhile to find out early on in the teaching of a group of students what their levels are in these aural aspects, and to give specific training in sound identification and discrimination, in listening with rapid comprehension and in literal discrimination.

3 *The problem of the medium*
It is easy enough, having acquired a skill, to forget what it was like in the

early stages of its acquisition: how hamfisted we were, how painfully slow, how inept in movement; and, perhaps most of all, in some skills like typewriting or scything, how tired we were after even a short concentrated effort. All this is applicable to the learner of a quick-writing system.

The problem for a Pitman 2000 teacher, for example, is that the learner has to acquire a writing skill which demands a quicker (and sometimes different) movement of the pen; and also, having more quickly reached a level of sophistication where he can (theoretically) write anything in English, the Pitman 2000 learner has had less time to cultivate this writing skill.

Provided that there is an early insistence on good penmanship—of which the basics are *lightness of touch, uniformity of size, correctness of outline* and *fluency of movement*—the Pitman Shorthand learner does not find writing a problem until 100 words a minute or above, and very often does not find it a problem even then. It is at this point, however, that the actual mechanics of getting the marks down on paper correctly and in the right places may begin to intrude themselves as a difficulty.

When a learner begins, some slow and incorrect movement is impossible to avoid. Psychologists show that we learn new skills like this by the process of trial and error, and by discarding what we find to be wrong and whittling our movements down to the correct ones until they become simultaneously habitual and fast. This empirical process needs to be speeded up, and the conscious endeavour to do the right thing stimulated by good teaching; the maximum effort has to be made early on to prevent a bad habit forming.

The teaching means at our disposal are:

> (*a*) Short verbal direction; guidance, encouragement, admonition. This can be general, as when you say, 'Write the circle **S** small and round', and individual, as when you say, 'Lift each finger a little clearer of the keys. Like this!'
> (*b*) Demonstration.
> (*c*) Repetition.

4 *Recency, frequency, intensity: the timetable problem*

We have explained that the most efficient and economical way of learning any skill that demands a fair amount of time for its acquisition is to work at it often, and to devote a relatively large amount of time to it within a relatively short space of calendar time.

To enlarge upon this. Short spells of 30–60 minutes, often repeated, produce a better result than spells of the same length or longer with intervals of days between. Three spells on Monday with two spells on Friday and nothing in between will produce a result only about a half or two-thirds as effective as one spell on each working day of the week. (It would work even better if we could get in one spell on each Saturday, Sunday and holiday too!) The psychological reason for this is that there is a sharp fall-away in attainment if a skill is left untouched for more than 24 hours. The mind forgets what to do; the muscles forget the habit pattern. Recency is a powerful factor in reinforcement.

On the other hand, a skill session continued too long will fairly quickly produce diminishing returns. How quickly this will happen depends on other factors—the temperament of the individual student and the level of motivation actuating the group. Properly conducted instruction in a time-skill will require a high level of effort and concentration from the learners, but this cannot be very long sustained: there is a need to separate one spell of effort from another.

This explains what is meant by the recency–frequency principle of skill learning. It would serve this principle if we had one 30–60 minute session each day; indeed, many current timetables are so arranged. But if you look at the overall learning of the skill you find that it may be still more efficiently and economically acquired if the total amount of learning time packed into a given period of, say, one month, is substantial.

The general results of the timetable situation for office skills as it exists in schools and colleges vary from excellent to absurd. In one college or school there may be 10 hours spread evenly over the week devoted to a skill, with short staggered periods. In another a teacher may be called upon to teach beginners a time-skill with two consecutive hours on Thursday, one on Friday, and none for the rest of the time.

The improvement of office-skills timetables must depend, as it largely does now, on the polite pressures and constant agitation of teachers themselves, the propagandizing work of the teachers' societies, the suggestions and advice of the specialists in the Department of Education and Science, and of the better understanding of the problems among those who face the administrative task.

5 *Memory: a learning problem*

In Pitman Shorthand—a symbolic writing system of subtlety, complexity and intellectual ingenuity—there is a considerable amount that has to be committed to memory and then practised to the point of automaticity. This apparent drawback to the system is in fact one of its great strengths, since the reduction in writing created by this moderately high memory load is phenomenally good—60 per cent and more of all words can be represented by a single stroke. But the system still has to be learned.

Equally, in learning typewriting there are, in addition to a number of manipulative operations into which we build skills, a substantial number of conventions and practices that affect particular typewriting outputs to be memorized.

James M. Thyne (op. cit.) has two relevant comments here: 'Since material which is meaningful and interesting to the learner is usually acquired faster and retained longer than is other material, it is profitable to try to ensure that the pupil understands what he has to memorize and is interested in it before he attempts to memorize it. By doing so, a teaching is in effect fulfilling the motivational requirement that the activity to be learned should be part of some wider activity in which the learner already engages. Since knowledge which the pupil finds rewarding to possess is likely to be retained longer, try to ensure that what he memorizes can be put to successful use.'

6 *Motivation: the pressure of time*

How keenly students desire to learn counts significantly in the speed and extent of their progress in acquiring a time-skill. Naturally, many students begin full of hope and keen to learn; equally naturally, many of them lose some or all of their original zest as they get into the subject.

The problem is more acute in time-skills than in other subjects since the learner has at every stage to face the fact that he must try to do what, at the moment of trying, he knows is beyond him. Much concentration and much effort is called for over and over again. The special problem of evening-class drop-outs is one reflection of this rapid seeping away of original purpose and resolve.

This is something that every teacher of office skills has to cope with, and successful teaching of these subjects may often depend on the manner in which the teacher surmounts it. The brilliant few manage not only to sustain the original motivation, but to increase it; even mediocre students can reach quite unexpected levels of attainment under such teachers.

How is it to be done? There is, of course, a natural genius in some teachers that cannot be taught or imitated. Here and there one observes with admiration the gifted teacher whose natural endowments provide a large part of the answer—one who seems able to establish an instant rapport with a class; whose antennae are forever attuned to the shifting moods and attitudes of the individuals in the group; who can vary speech, approach and method to suit every circumstance, and who can carry the class along on a wave of continuous, enjoyable and productive activity.

Nevertheless, there is much that the rest of us can do, aided by our own conscientiousness and the accumulated experience of the successful teachers. The more important of those factors that sustain motivation are listed below:

(*a*) Planning and preparation. If it is apparent that you have 'done your homework' and know exactly what you are going to do next, a class will always know and appreciate this. Students who are aware that pains are being taken in their interests will generally respond. It has to be remembered, though, that no plan ought to be regarded as inflexible; even experienced teachers can easily make mistakes in judging what the response and progress of a class is likely to be. You have to be ready to adjust and modify your original plan.

(*b*) One learning activity continued for too long can quickly run away with interest and effort. So too can the same *pattern* of activities—even if it is a good one—repeated through session after session of instruction. So a variety of programme helps to keep interest alive and effort sustained.

(*c*) In the group learning situation one always has to be aware that one is teaching a class, and that one is simultaneously helping individuals to learn. Individuals are not alike: their attitudes, temperaments and difficulties vary. Knowing each member of the group well, and providing judiciously just that measure of help and guidance that will assist each one to do better, is a contributory factor to the overall level of motivation of the group.

(*d*) Planning for success is vital. Any activity which, when assessed, shows half of the class to be failures, is a disaster and one must look immediately for the reasons. Was it too difficult? Was the time too short? Was it not clear enough what was to be done? Had they not learned enough in order to do it? Did I teach them in the right way? Did I conduct the activity incorrectly? Success has to be marked overtly and demonstrably; it has to be underlined. Any student (that is, any one of us) who has the experience *I did quite well on that. With a little more of X or a little more of Y, I shall do better still* has the psychological reinforcement of success. In this frame of mind it is easy to induce students to go on and maintain the level of their effort and attention.

(*e*) A very important element in motivation is the degree to which the individual learners understand what is going on. Every activity in a time-skill should be meaningful. The student has every right to know—indeed *must* know—if real success is to be achieved: *Why am I doing this? What ought the end result to be? How long have I to do it? Exactly how should I do it? How does it contribute to my long-term goals?* So every target of training has to be meaningful to learners. This is the way to avoid the monotony or boredom that, under the wrong conditions, may result from repetition.

(*f*) In one way we have already thought about the qualities of the teacher as being of great importance in maintaining, or even increasing, motivation. But apart from the natural endowments previously mentioned, much can be achieved in this line simply by working at it. Office-skills teachers need, and usually have, a considerable enthusiasm for their subjects and this, if genuine and not too histrionically exhibited, will also enthuse the students. The energy—or what footballers call 'the work-rate'—is similarly a strong motivating factor. The teacher's apparent ability to be in several places at once and to know everything that is going on gains not only student respect but student co-operation; to this should be added the permanent attitude of encouragement and help. Exhortations, acid strictures on students' work or attitudes, the constant negative *Don't . . .*, grumbles and complaints—all of these will not get very far at all. The positive, cheerful, encouraging attitude is far more likely to get a positive, cheerful result.

(*g*) What has just been said does not imply that students are always right, nor that the standards they set for themselves are necessarily acceptable. The truth is that in time-skills the setting of high standards, showing how to reach them, and then insisting on their performance, will better motivate students and make them far readier to carry on than if a general sloppiness prevails. Have you observed, for example, that the outstandingly successful teachers in typewriting are nearly always those who have a touch of the martinet in their constitution and yet are always totally involved in the work and performance of each individual student? Yet students who work with such teachers often have extraordinarily high motivation and—to put it colloquially—eat out of their hands. A classic instance I have in mind is of a very gifted teacher who ran a special after-hours class for students 'who really wanted to get on' and who had, not just every place taken, but a permanent waiting list of students eager to get in!

The corollary to the setting of standards is the requirement of work. Perhaps some people are more work-shy than they were a few decades ago, but there could be many reasons for that which are not connected with the character or values-sense of the student. Fortunately, the majority of students are quite ready to work—and work very hard—if they see clearly and understand the reasons for it. One apparently paradoxical way of keeping motivation high is to demand hard work out of the students and to see that you get it.

In the time-skills, pressure of time is often at the root of loss of interest and effort—I mean pressure of time in the sense that much of the work needed has to be done with one eye on the watch. From the learner's viewpoint this has a dual aspect of attraction and repulsion: it attracts because everyone likes the challenge of trying to succeed against the clock; it repels because it is wearying. We can remind ourselves just how wearying by trying to take dictation at 10 words a minute above our comfortable speed for three or four three-minute sessions. One needs a strong shot of motivation to keep it up. This particular difficulty is also concerned with repetition and what reactions that may cause, and that is a topic we shall now discuss.

7 Repetition

How we learn is still an open field for exploration and research. We know much more about it than we did 30 or 40 years ago, but we also know that there is still much that we do not know. But that repetitive work is an indispensable constituent of skills acquisition is an inescapable fact of life. Fortunately, repetition of itself is not an uncongenial human activity: it can be both pleasurable and satisfying as it is in music, poetry or dancing. It only becomes uncongenial when carried on too long or when it is sapped of its purpose and meaning. It is this that is the core of the problem in the acquisition of time-skills: a great deal of repetition is called for. An average session of instruction may well contain half or more of repetitive activity of one kind or another, and that is a high proportion; then we hear that it becomes boring or monotonous and so dissipates interest and effort, although there is no need for such a situation to arise.

In a sense the difficulty is, I suppose, that although we can observe what the learner is doing or saying we cannot get inside his mind to find out what is going on in there. If practice is mechanical and mindless, progress is at a halt; we have to persuade learners to think what they are doing all the time. The first step in this process is that at each repetition called for, they should know precisely and unambiguously why they are doing this particular job. The second step is to find some means of getting the learners to use their minds on the job, and not to slip into a heedless and unthinking repetition. 'Practice makes perfect' only when the practice is guided, defined, given a goal and passes through the conscious mind.

There are a number of teaching devices for keeping students' minds on the job of repetition. For example, in shorthand:

(*a*) In dictated copying, call upon individual students to say the form they have just written or the form that comes next.

(*b*) Make slight variations in the words or the order of the words, just sufficiently to keep the group on the alert.

(*c*) Vary the order when short sentences are being repeated. Do not necessarily keep to 1, 2, 3 . . .

(*d*) Have each 10 or 20 words repeated aloud from the students' notes before going on.

(*e*) Occasionally repeat certain words and phrases so that the student writes them twice.

(*f*) When reading and re-reading is the activity, use the 'one pen lift' technique of reading round the class, each student reading one word or one group of words written without a lift of the pen. A little experience will soon make this a fast and stimulating exercise with everybody thinking and alert.

(*g*) When more continuous reading aloud is the activity, and individual students are reading ten or a dozen words, have each successive one called upon pick up four or five words from what has just been read before going on, like this:

I may go to the sea. I enjoy a picnic by the sea picnic by the sea when the sea is calm we enjoy a picnic we enjoy a picnic up on the common. We see the sunlight, etc.

(*h*) Use timed reading with a stopwatch and assess a reading speed for each student in words a minute. It also helps sometimes to change the goals during a particular repetition, e.g. accuracy of writing, speed of writing, rising speeds of copying over a short take (20–30 words), speed of reading back from the student's own note, and so on.

Using such methods will soon set a standard. Students will realize that when they are engaged on repetition they must have their minds switched on at all times if they are going to attain the standard required. The result will be that the risk of monotony and its concomitant—non-learning—will very largely be obviated. Repetition will be seen to be a highway to the acquisition of the skill.

8 *Unequal attainment*

A difficulty that often arises as soon as the beginning stage is over is that of unequal progress: some students show immediate aptitude and go rapidly ahead; others lag far behind. In skills where so much depends on time and speed, this situation can be a serious problem for student and teacher.

Where forty or more students begin at the same time, there is a workable solution in grading which can begin as early as at the end of twenty or thirty hours and have a built-in flexibility thereafter on approximately a once-a-month basis. Some schools and colleges with large numbers of beginners even carry this effective system into the 'theory' stage and have a series of three or four hurdles for students to get over in order to progress to the next group; if they fail, they take the section again. Usually, however, divergence in attainment does not show itself as too sharp a problem until speed development; then it can sometimes become acute.

What can be done about a class of twenty with a speed range of 40 wam in shorthand and 20 wam in typewriting? In shorthand, at least, whatever you do you cannot meet the needs of all the students all the time; you can only try to meet the needs of most of the students most of the time. Here are some of these expedients:

(*a*) Group teaching. The class is divided into two or even three groups according to ability, and the teacher switches maximum attention from one group to another in turn, while ensuring that the group(s) not being attended to is (are) occupied in worthwhile activity and study. Such a method of instruction is very hard, but there are some teachers who can manage it with considerable success (see also (10) below).

(*b*) Use of individual playback facilities. Where there is good provision of audio material and equipment, it is possible to hive off at different times the slower students and the 'flyers' separately, so that teaching of the non-audio group may continue.

(*c*) The slower students may be asked to use audio facilities after normal hours of study in order to catch up. If this is done, it is very important that the work should be carefully planned and supervised. To realize that you are below the class average and a long way below the 'flyers' is a very discouraging thing. Unless such students are given maximum help and sincere encouragement they are probable drop-outs. One has to emphasize over and over again that the history of skills teaching is full of instances of students who may well have been written off as failures at one stage but who have persisted to become top-rank skills operatives.

(*d*) Whatever is done in this situation, it is still very important to devote a good proportion of the time to class teaching with everybody working together. A class generates its own communal spirit which is normally of high value to each individual, and it is important to maintain this. In this case, one has to be judicious about questioning and cut one's coat according to the student's cloth. Equally, one has to be judicious about the kinds of activity required of the class, so that the slower student can win a measure of success at his level and the 'flyer' a measure of success at his.

(e) If the individual relationships in the class are well enough known, it can be helpful to pair students so that the weaker one can get unobtrusive help. The protégé system can be highly effective.

(f) If the gaps in attainment are not too wide, the class can still be kept together if the less able students are required—and agree—to do more specific preparation, preview and writing exercises on their own for each period of instruction. In typewriting the problems of divergence in attainment are less acute. The capable teacher can, on the same basic material, often allow for two or three different and approximately comparable groups to work at different practices in which length is the criterion, so that each, if properly allocated, will finish at about the same time. In the important speed–accuracy–plain copy area of typewriting work, the kind of system described in the chapter on teaching typewriting, which allows for wholly individual work to go on under a class system of organization, will adequately cater for differences in level of attainment.

9 *The group versus the individual*

In teaching office skills every teacher has to cope with the difficulty that the demands on time are always greater than the time available: one would like to spend more time with Jane or Susan, but that would lead to the group as a whole being neglected. Therefore a kind of balance has to be worked out between the two contending forces of attention to the class and attention to the individual.

Too much attention devoted to individuals is as much a risk as too little. A group very often works better as a group when the individuals can feel that they are engaged in a communal and purposeful activity (see (d) above). On the other hand, giving too little attention to individuals risks widening the gap between those with immediate natural aptitude and those who need coaching, guidance and encouragement.

It is all a question of judgement, both in the short-term and in the long-term situation. You have to judge by the signs in the short-term situation whether you are spending too much time continuously on individuals: the signs will probably be a slackening of effort, a diminution in interest, conversation, diversionary activities and some impatience manifested perhaps by physical movement or an irrelevant question. Equally, in the long-term situation you have to judge whether you are giving enough attention to some individuals by the cumulative results of the work of the class. It may even be necessary, as was mentioned earlier, to give out-of-class time to the special problems of some individuals.

10 *Class, group and individual teaching*

You are a teacher of the office skills and you are about to begin your task in your place of work. What kind of situation may you find yourself in? You will, it is hoped, have a separate place to work, which will be endowed with environmental conditions that may vary from the barely tolerable to the ideal, and with books, equipment, materials and teaching aids that may vary from the grotesquely inadequate to the breathtakingly super-abundant. These words are chosen with care: they are based upon experience in a dozen different English-speaking countries.

Into this place will come people—students—rarely all at once: some will be late (10 minutes or three weeks), some early; some will be away from class for hours, days, or weeks. Few will be present at each and every class.

These students will differ in age, sex, aptitude, ability and temperament: some may be eager and ready to learn; others may be dully apathetic. Some, even, may be there for reasons that have no educational justification or reason at all.

Your task is to impart this skill to all of them as best you can. How are you to cope?

One way is to adopt a rigid class-teaching system which treats all students alike and requires them all to follow precisely the same learning and activities at the same time. The system has merits: if it is properly done, a helpful class spirit will be created; students will derive much from one another; the majority will learn; discipline, administration, effective command of the learning situation are all easier. The trouble is that class teaching of this type is unfair to two groups: those at the top will soon be working below their potential; those at the bottom will be floundering. Your teaching, aimed as it must be at the average, cannot cater for their special needs. Also, you will find a disproportionate amount of your time will have to be devoted to correction, remedial work and revision.

Another way is that already described in (9) in which the class is divided, when their lack of homogeneity begins to become obtrusive, into two or three groups according to their level of attainment. Then you concentrate about an equal amount of your available time on each of the groups, leaving those not being specifically attended to some tasks based on their last group session. One advantage is that teacher–student contact is closer; a second is that the special needs of the high-flyers and the laggards are catered for. The drawbacks are severe: much greater demands are made upon the teacher in terms of preparation and adjustment to needs; students left to their own devices soon lose the drive that often the teacher alone can instil; the students become fractious, frustrated; their work-rate will suffer a marked drop. Moreover, they will soon cease to be a class and may become a rabble.

Still another way is, apart from a brief period of initial teaching, to devote all the time to individuals. Here the same drawbacks as in group teaching operate still more intensively. Students lose all the benefit of stimulation through exchange of ideas, question and answer, emulation and rivalry, and of learning from one another. Each student can only hope for a very short period of individual attention and everybody works at a slower rate. Many students will reach some crux point and be unable to go on without help. Wrong habits will creep in and incorrect work will be done. Resentment and indiscipline will soon appear.

Without the flexibility of large numbers to permit of a re-arrangement of classes to secure homogeneity, there is only a compromise solution. However, this compromise can be made to work reasonably well. Class teaching of time-skills has the most in its favour, so adopt that for most of the time. For short periods go into a group arrangement giving the greater part of your attention to the brightest students as they will get most out of it. When the class is working together at some whole-class activity then give your individual attention to the weaker members of the class. Clearly this method calls for careful preparation and considerable versatility on the part of the teacher but, assuming that you do the former and that you possess, or can attain to, the latter, then it is the only way to meet the problem. There will be a very few (some of whom I have seen and admired) who can work the group system and surmount its limitations. There will be a few more who are only at their best using the whole-class system. But most teachers will achieve their best results using the system advocated.

5 Teaching Typewriting

The continuous rise in the demand for business records and communication has led to an increasing reliance on typewriting as the most important office skill. Not only has the demand for quick and efficient typewriting risen throughout this century, and at a faster rate in the last twenty years, but it has been given new and important applications such as the setting of type for printing, the teleprinter and the input to computer out-stations.

It is a pity that the machine itself, a highly sophisticated and beautifully engineered device, should—so far as its keyboard is concerned—be almost as bad as could be devised (see p. 7).

The demand for good teachers of typewriting has for many years past outstripped the facilities available for training such teachers and, in addition, the number of suitably qualified persons coming forward for teacher training has also, for various reasons, been far fewer than needed.

Typewriting-room equipment

A particular room for teaching typewriting is essential, as the instruction demands specialized equipment and furniture. All of the following items are desirable, some are indispensable:

Tables or working surfaces: these should provide ample space for laying out the various items that will be necessary, especially in transcription work or in a continuous project. The surfaces should average 711 mm (28 in.) from the floor but there should be some both higher and lower than this; adjustable typing chairs.

Stationery and stationery store: A4, A5 and other paper sizes. Letterheads, carbons, backing sheets, envelopes, memorandum forms, printed forms etc.

Typewriters and copyholders: if only one typewriting room is available it will be necessary to have two-thirds of the machines identical, the remainder made up of various other types. One-quarter of them should be electric, since it is essential that all learners should gain adequate experience on both manual and electric machines. If there is more than one room, one should be wholly equipped with electric machines of the same model. It will also be necessary for the students to have experience on both elite and pica-type keyboards.

Demonstration stand; rotary and spirit duplicators; photocopiers; filing cabinets; bookshelf with reference books; audio transcribers; cassette player and/or tape recorder.

Ancillary machines: guillotine, stapler, punch, pencil sharpener, collator, shredder, electronic calculator, adhesive-tape dispenser, gum moistener.

Bulletin (display) board; plastograph board; overhead projector; lettering stencils (Letraset, Econasign); chalkboard; large timing clock clearly visible from any station in the room; wall maps and charts.

Typewriting-room organization

Because of the demand for typewriting instruction it is common to have 25 or more stations in the one room. While this is not too serious a drawback at the keyboard-learning stage, it is far too many during production-typewriting activities. The constant use of the room, usually by day and evening too, demands a high degree of maintenance and systematic attention to order, neatness and safety. Adequate space is essential to allow the teacher to move freely round the room in order to watch and help each individual student. A Repairs Book listing the place, serial number, make of machine, fault, repair date and check should be systematically kept.

Activities during the acquisition of typewriting skill

A wide range of sub-skills and items of knowledge have to be acquired before one becomes an accomplished typist. Basically, however, learning to type divides itself into:

(a) Learning to use the keyboard and the manipulative devices of the typewriter with increasing speed and accuracy.

(b) Learning to produce the various kinds of documents and records that are demanded by business according to the prescriptions of convention, custom and commonsense.

Modern thinking about this is generally in favour of conducting both kinds of activity—the specific keyboard practice and the production typewriting—side by side. On the other hand, there is a doubt about what level of manipulative skill ought to be reached before the production of typewritten documents according to formula is required. Until machine handling and confident key-striking have been attained at a copy speed of about 25 wam, the introduction of specific production exercises is likely to be unsuccessful.

Some teachers pay little attention to machine-manipulation practice once this stage of confidence is reached, their viewpoint being that students will acquire higher speed and greater accuracy from their production-work practice. No doubt this is to a large extent true. For all that, most learner-typists are not in fact coached towards their true potential in keyboard speed and reduction of error. It is likely to lead to a more effective result if the plain-copy element, which enables the learner to concentrate on her speed and accuracy only, is retained as an essential short daily activity all through the course of training.

The table that follows is an indication of the order in which the typewriter work that has to be included in a livelihood-earning course might be presented. But before that, it has to be remembered that what makes a particular typewriting exercise difficult or easy is not only its own nature. Other factors that greatly affect this are:

The input medium (manuscript, typescript, print, corrected input of these types; shorthand, voice recording—audio).

Degree of modification and correction; quality of the written or dictated input.

Length: it may be said here that while this is an undoubted factor in difficulty it is also a factor in practice. Most practice exercises are too long. Students benefit most from a repetition of the sub-skill they have just acquired in several slightly different ways. Three or four short practices will be both more motivating and interesting and will achieve better learning than one long one. Textbook exercises can often be cut down with advantage.

Degree of difficulty inherent in the material: the vocabulary, content, use of figures, formulae, abbreviations, awkward displayed matter etc.

Extent of deviation needed from the original copy: has the whole arrangement to be changed? Has fresh material to be brought in from elsewhere?

Copies needed; time available.

Typewriting Instruction Presentation

Subject matter	*Suitable material*
STAGE 1	
Learning to operate the machine: key positions; fingering; striking technique; posture; paper insertion and removal; shift lock; figures	Words Phrases Sentences (exercising cumulatively keys and reaches taught)
Parts of typewriter	
Chief punctuation conventions	
STAGE 2	
Extension of keyboard mastery	Sentences
All characters and combinations	Paragraphs (with figures and other characters)
Figures; margins; line ends; hyphens, dashes, parentheses, quotes, underscores	Brief articles Pacing drills Brief anecdotes
Paragraphing	Informative paragraphs (typing information)
Speed and accuracy development	
Erasing (as soon as first production work is encountered)	
STAGE 3	
Input from: simple uncorrected typescript, manuscript, print, accurate chalkboard shorthand	Easy letters and memorandums Short notices and directives Forms Simple minutes
Elementary matters of judgement and placement	Simple tables Standard business documents: invoices, statements, orders, requisitions, credit and delivery notes, telephone messages
Centring	
Side headings	
Equal columns	
Completion of printed forms	Simplified block layout applied throughout
Continuation sheets	
Using carbons	
Centring to given margins and to page	
Introduction of audio-typing	
Speed and accuracy development	

Subject matter   *Suitable material*

STAGE 4

Input from corrected and amended typescript, print, manuscript, facsimile shorthand, shorthand notes, audio tape/cassette etc.	Letters (with internal tabulation)
	More difficult examples of the standard business documents
Problems of judgement and placement	Agendas
Unequal columns	Minutes
Display	Programmes
Extension of simplified block layout into all types of typewriting	Schedules
	Itineraries
	Statistical tables
Preparation of masters for photocopying, rotary and spirit duplicators, offset	Financial statements
	Reports (with sectional and sub-headings)
Ruling	Specialized technical work: wills, specifications, etc. (if these are needed in the course)
Vertical headings	
Matching pages	
Preparing 4- or 6-page leaflets and gatefolds	
Continuous topic documents	
Space and wordage calculations	
Typing from brief notes and originator's instructions	

Typewriting teaching principles re-examined

The teaching of typewriting is still conducted on the basis of assumptions, some of which are demonstrably false or partially so. These will now be considered in turn, the teaching implications being obvious, it is hoped, from what is said. The attack on unjustifiable assumptions is mainly the work of Leonard West in the USA, and his book, *Acquisition of Typewriting Skills* (Pitman), is the most definitive and detailed examination of every aspect of typewriting and of the research that has led to the consideration of new answers to many teaching problems.

(a) Touch typing
Touch typing is rightly considered to be an aim of all modern teaching. In effect, this means that ultimately the typist will know how to strike

each key on the typewriter, upper and lower case, without the need to look in order to locate the key and with the correct fingering for each such key-stroke in-built as a permanent habit. Two assumptions have been made: the first is that the fingering as we have it at this time is the 'correct' (the most efficient) one, and secondly that the way towards building this habit is to prevent the learner from visually locating the keys, even at the very outset. To achieve this aim typewriters were (in some places, still are) provided with blank keys, and other devices such as keyboard shields and aprons were used to stop the learner from their instinctive and natural attempts to locate keys by sight. It is now much more generally accepted that the most potent sensory input of sight is essential as a first stage in building up instinctive key-location and fingering habits; teaching nowadays tends to shift the emphasis to sight location and fingering until such time as the habit has become established. Step-by-step the student is led away progressively from visual to tactile operation. In figure work, it is true that even the expert typist continues to look and indeed will from time to time check her touch-typing habit by a quick glance at the keys to reinforce her kinaesthetic sense.

(b) Speed and accuracy

It is now more generally recognized that all attempts to secure accuracy by concentrating solely on it as the only worthwhile goal in the early stages of typewriting learning is a self-defeating exercise.

Such practice requirements as three perfect sentence copies before proceeding to the next drill are seen to be utterly dis-motivating and productive of reactive inhibition and stagnation in progress. In the early stages of learning it is the technique that is important; the 'how' is much more productive than the 'what'. Frequent errors are unavoidable when the learner is still groping to acquire the right habit and an insistence on perfection in the typed copy produces a negative result.

Similarly, it is now much more widely understood that the two necessary goals of speed and accuracy are not compatible during the learning period. The most effective learning comes when the goals are kept apart and the learner aims first for speed of operation and then—having made some progress along this path—switches the aim to accuracy.

Furthermore, an undue pressure for speed will result in a breakdown of technique and of achievement. The aim to secure quick typing must be controlled by pacing techniques so that the speed-of-movement goal does not break down under pressure: students who learn by an initial emphasis on speed become, in the end, much faster but equally accurate typists. This has been realized for longer in North America than in Great Britain, with the result that American typists are (possibly for this reason) commonly 5–10 wam faster than ours.

In the early stages more time has to be spent on correctness of technique and the drive for speed than in being accurate; accuracy becomes a by-product of the forward march of speed. Only when the chains in key-striking of the most frequent literal patterns in the English language have been built up and the correct fingering has become instinctive, can we then devote more time to shedding the physical sensory-motor imperfections that result in mistakes. There is more to it than this, of course, and the matter will be more fully considered in the section on errors (see p. 67 *et seq.*).

(c) Common word and low syllabic intensity material for early practice
It is often thought helpful to learners to give them very simple material to practise on at first—material on a restricted vocabulary of 700–1,000 words and sentences that are in the main monosyllabic and rarely exceed 3 or 4 strokes per word. On the face of it this seems a reasonable argument, but in fact it is based on assumptions probably drawn from shorthand but not applicable to typewriting.

It has been shown that even the expert typist rarely produces a built-in response pattern for more than three letters at a time. There may well be a few five-letter responses to prompts like 'there' or 'lands' but these do not change the dominant digram–trigram pattern. We know from research what, in fact, these common letter collocations are. This is the frequency table:

Commonest English

Digrams	Trigrams
TH	THE
HE	AND
IN	ING
ER	ION
AN	ENT
RE	TIO
ON	HER
AT	FOR
EN	HAT
ND	THA
ED	HIS
OR	TER

The common, easy words will get all the practice that they require from the mere fact that they recur unavoidably in any average English material. The main aim of keyboard work must be to establish as quickly as possible these digrams and trigrams that introduce about half of the alphabet, but a further point is that they may be preceded or followed by any other letters. It is in first establishing the digrams and trigrams as patterns, and then using them in the context of any surrounding letters, which will necessitate a sort of 'getting-ready' technique that produces the expert typist.

There is, therefore, no reason at all why the learner should not use material of unrestricted vocabulary (consonant, of course, with their comprehension) and there is equally no reason why they should be called upon to repeat the same material, except perhaps in the switching of goals from speed to accuracy where the slight familiarity built up may stand the learner in good stead when it comes to aiming at the minimum number of mistakes.

(d) Development of rhythm
There is value in the early stages of learning in requiring students to type at a fixed pace of striking with an equal time interval between one stroke and the next. But in a short time, the learner will begin to type combinations like e-r, i-n, t-h, b-y and even 'and' and 'the' as a unit. At that stage, metronomic typing ceases to have any instructional value, and in the opinion of the author should be dropped. Music from records or cassettes has this early and occasional merit of persuading the students to concentrate on correct key-striking—it may also help the learner to get the right 'mind-set' and not try to push too hard for speed—and it is of itself mildly motivating, but its value soon fades. From the time the student has reasonable confidence in typing at 20 wam or above, all over the keyboard, music and metronomic typing having nothing further to contribute.

It is common to hear rhythm discussed as characteristic of a good typist; indeed, it appears, extraordinarily enough, in the syllabuses of examinations. To say what it means is both impossible and unnecessary; all learners will, in fact, find out their own most effective patterns of motion. When these are listened to or recorded (as in Diatype or in the work done by D. W. Hardy in the early 1930s (see 'Rhythmisation and Speed of Work', *British Journal of Psychology*, 1932)) what emerges is that the expert typist leaves crisp, clear-cut but very tiny intervals between strikes, and that these form quick–slow patterns according to the ease or difficulty of the motions entailed. The order of difficulty can be stated to be, from the hardest, same finger, near finger, far finger, opposite hand, index fingers on opposite hands.

Any attempt, therefore, to impose an equal inter-stroke interval on learners is not only doomed to failure, it is also regressive: rhythm drills are a pointless waste of time.

This leaves the question of what is typewriting rhythm unanswered, beyond what may be inferred by this analysis; and needless anyway.

(e) Reading skill: the work of Lillian Malt

The original contribution made by Lillian Malt to research into keyboard training and the theory of typewriting should be better known. She has concentrated mostly on the industrial and, in particular, the printing applications of keyboard work. The experiments that she conducted have clearly shown that there is a very direct relationship between the speed and accuracy of reading from copy and the speed and accuracy of keyboarding. People who are trained to read faster and with wider comprehension also type faster.

The goal of the skills-analysis courses of training that run along these lines is 24 000 keystrokes an hour, i.e. 80 wam, and this is regarded as the norm of professional attainment. During the actual instruction, a part of which is always devoted to the improvement of reading skills, the other main areas of emphasis are:

(i) accuracy comes from correctness of movement not from correction of error;

(ii) the habit patterns based on the main digrams and trigrams have to be automaticized. Therefore the practice material concentrates on these;

(iii) environmental assistance to concentration is necessary;

(iv) correctness and speed of striking is a vital element from the beginning.

All of these elements would be endorsed today by many successful typewriting teachers.

Most of the rest of this chapter can be divided into a closer consideration of the two main divisions of typewriter manipulation and production typewriting. Although we are looking at them separately they do in fact overlap during a typewriting course, although to what extent is still a debatable matter. Some, like Leonard West, advocate the earliest introduction of production typewriting and a lower level of concentration on sheer keyboarding skill. The view of the author is that, since it is demonstrable that in the UK at least, students do not generally reach anything like their potential in terms of sheer speed plus accuracy, and equally that the level of attainment in keyboarding does have an effect upon production typewriting, it is preferable in a short (40-week or less) course to include specific keyboard training of 10–20 minutes in every period each or every other day after students have reached 25 wam, and more before that.

Typewriter manipulation

The keyboard

Typewriters with English keyboards come in all shapes and sizes and with a variety of different control devices. Fundamentally, however, they are divided into manually- or electrically-operated mechanisms, into pica or elite types (a number of different typefaces being available in each of these kinds) and with standard or long carriages. Even the arrangement of keys may differ slightly from one keyboard to another; however, the main alphabetic arrangement is the same everywhere. The British Standards Institution has been co-operating with other national bodies in order to set up standard international layouts for various purposes and interested teachers should consult the Institution at: 2 Park Street, London W 1.

Today the electric typewriter prevails, the number of these machines sold in the UK exceeding the number of manual ones for the first time in 1972; in the USA this has been so for several years longer. In the end, consideration will have to be given to teaching learners on electric typewriters from the beginning and comparative experiments along this line, with interesting and useful results, were conducted by Rosemary Harris, formerly Principal of the Langham Secretarial College.

However, most learners in the UK still begin on manual machines and, if they are fortunate, graduate on to electric ones later in their course or when they go out to earn their living as typists. The transition is not very difficult, usually taking two to three weeks.

The keyboard itself remains virtually unchanged since the original commercial machine produced by C. Latham Scholes in 1873. It is notoriously and grossly inefficient in terms of the arrangement of keys, the most frequently-used letters and letter combinations often offering the greatest element of difficulty and a considerable imbalance existing between the work of the individual fingers and the hands.

Fifty years ago, after long research, August Dvorak produced a vastly improved key arrangement and spent years unsuccessfully trying to get his work accepted and generally adopted. This is the Dvorak keyboard:

DVORAK

```
7   5   3   1   9   0   2   4   6   8
?   ,   .   P   Y   F   G   C   R   L
A   O   E   U   I   D   H   T   N   S
    Q   J   K   X   B   M   W   V   Z
```

Charles Lekberg in the *Saturday Review* in September 1972 wrote an article on this subject entitled: 'How a hundred-year-old typing system can tangle your fingers and waste your time.' He says: 'On the Dvorak keyboard you can type more than 3,000 common words on the familiar home row (A O E U I D H T N S) compared with only about fifty on QWERTY's home row. Dvorak put all the vowels in this row under the fingers of the left hand. The right hand rested atop H T N and S with D just to the left of the right index finger. . . . Dvorak rearranged things so that 70 per cent of the work could be done on the home row, 22 per cent on the upper row and only 8 per cent below.'

On QWERTY 32 per cent is done on the home row, 52 per cent above and 16 per cent below. The left hand on the QWERTY board gets 57 per cent of the load and the right hand 43 per cent. Dvorak shifted this weighting to 56 per cent right hand, 44 per cent left hand.

It is also interesting to note that there is, as would be expected, a close correspondence here with letter frequency. The frequency of letters in ordinary English material is as follows if E, the commonest letter, is taken as 100:

E	100	R	44
T	69	H	40
N	50	L	28
S	47	D	26

Only **R** and **L** are *not* on the Dvorak home row and they are both to be found in the easier upper row. A final point is that in using the Dvorak keyboard the finger load is much more equally distributed, as follows:

	Left				*Right*			
	4	3	2	1	1	2	3	4
QWERTY	8·2	7·9	18·4	22·9	21·6	7·2	12·6	1·3
DVORAK	8·1	8·8	12·8	14·2	18·5	15·3	13·4	8·9

In 1965 the United States Bureau of Standards said: 'There is little need to demonstrate further the superiority of the Dvorak keyboard in experimental tests. Plenty of well-documented evidence exists already.'

In general Dvorak's experiments show a more than 50 per cent increase in output and accuracy.

There seem the strongest arguments why the Dvorak keyboard should be introduced with a possible re-arrangement of fingering so as to reduce still further or entirely eliminate the use of the little (and weakest) fingers.

Learning the keyboard

It may be confidently stated that the first two or three weeks of learning to type are more important than any other in the course. During this period the students have to learn the location of each character, what finger to use, how to strike the keys, how to insert, remove and align paper, how to return the carriage, how to set margins and how to sequence their movements so as to attain speed of operation with economy of physical action.

Striking technique

Of these activities the manner of striking the keys is unquestionably the most important, since building the right habits in this area will favourably affect everything that is done afterwards. Here I quote the words of Janet Malempre, a London principal, who has studied typing technique here and in North America. She says: 'Good striking technique must be taught from the first lesson. Teachers should demonstrate how to strike a key with a sharp staccato touch. The fingers should be loosely curled and relaxed. The emphasis in the practice should be for a high striking rate; accuracy is subsidiary at this stage. Students should be told and shown by chart or OHP which key they have to hit and with which finger. Then they should look at that key and make a few experimental movements from the anchor position to 'get the feel' of the necessary motion, then they should strike on the command of the teacher and as sharply (but *not* heavily) as they can.

'The keys to be practised should be called at regular intervals, the voice inflection indicating the need for swift, crisp movement. After a short practice of this kind, the students should practise at their own rate.'

This early practice is best done from chalkboard or OHP because by this means the student is encouraged to keep her eyes on the copy rather than on the keys or the typing line. On the other hand, no attempt should be made to prevent students from looking; checking back on to type line is necessary after every 10–15 strikes in order to ensure the correct motion is being made. Janet Malempre goes on to say: 'Correct striking is often neglected or given insufficient attention in teaching, even by those who are very thorough in other matters. Its neglect is serious even for a short time, for it will give rise to errors and to slower progress which comes from students relying too much on trial and error.'

To encourage the link between character and action the letters, as they are struck, should be quietly spoken aloud.

Criteria of keyboard learning

(i) *How long to cover the keyboard?* How long to spend on covering all the keyboard characters and activities is not something that can be dogmatized about. The natural ability of the students must affect this decision. However, it can be said that the quicker the coverage, other things being equal, the better. It is necessary to get on to the known pattern of digrams and trigrams as quickly as possible, and until the whole keyboard has been covered this cannot be done. I have heard from Rewa Begg in New Zealand of a successful experiment in covering the alphabetic board (without shift) in one hour, but this would be exceptional. For students of average ability, about seven or eight 45-minute periods will work with three, four or five keys introduced at a time, depending upon their ease of striking and frequency order.

Thereafter, consolidation on unrestricted average English material is needed.

(ii) *What sequence of letters?* Two basic methods for the introduction of the keys are the *horizontal* and the *vertical*. In the horizontal method the home row is first learned, then the upper bank, then the lower bank, lastly the top bank. The possible advantages of this method are: all fingers are used from the start; the hand position is established by using the '**a**' and '**;**' as the anchor positions; correct striking technique is built before reaches have to be tackled.

In the vertical method, the keys are learned in files. The advocates of this method, increasing in number, are able to point to these possible advantages: use of the stronger fingers first and, since the reaches are easier, we are using the good teaching principle of proceeding from the simple to the more difficult; the use of two fingers on four keys is easier to establish as a habit than that of four fingers on four keys; since the vowels come in sooner by this method, it is easier to create meaningful material in words and sentences.

But these methods are not the only ones. Perhaps the principles on which judgement should finally be made are these:

Never teach adjacent keys at the same time

Never teach two similar reaches on the same fingers of either hand at the same time

These are really important points since their neglect is known to be fruitful of error (see p. 67 *et seq*.):

Initial ease of striking (therefore index and second fingers)
Establishment of correct striking technique (therefore home row)
Early introduction of frequent letters (**E, T, A, O, I, N, S, R, H, L, D**) to assist in composing the right material

The author therefore follows Grace McNicol in advocating a combination of approaches, viz. the home row followed by 'skip-around' which takes into account the other principles mentioned above.

Leonard West, while agreeing that in the fairly short term, one method is not much more advantageous than another provided that the 'never' provisos mentioned above are observed, suggests the following pattern:

1. i, f, s, t, . , shift	5. y b p
2. a k l h e	6. j w u
3. v o d	7. x z c n q
4. g r m	

(iii) *Repeated demonstration* At this stage more than any other, good and repeated demonstrations are essential for the learner's progress, even at the level of individual demonstration when the teacher, who should act all the time as a coach and exemplar, sees an immediate need.

(iv) *What should the learner's posture be?* The relationship of the learner's hands and forearms to the keyboard and the working surface are the really important things. From long experience it seems that if the operator is to be in command of the machine, and not vice versa, the forearms should be parallel with the floor or even slightly down-sloping to the keyboard. The sit-up-and-beg position will certainly reduce command and be a source of error. The hands have to be kept as motionless as possible, though this is not to be pushed to absurd lengths: hand movement is necessary especially in the stage when the keying is 'chained' and the operator, while typing one key, is already making preparatory adjustments for the next two. The anchor positions of the little fingers should always be apparent so that 'return' is as important as 'move' in finger movements.

All the rest is subordinate and contributes more to comfort and 'mind-set' than to actual typing speed and accuracy. Of course it is helpful to sit well back in an adjustable chair, not too close to the machine. The demand for the students to keep elbows tucked in seems to achieve nothing except inhibition; expert typists are always making slight movements of their elbows in order to shift their hands into command positions. The hands and fingers need to be kept close to the keys, and the common fault of maestro-piano-playing with the hands performing a balletic movement over the board should be checked as soon as it appears. Of course, it helps also to be in a position where the feet can be firmly planted on the floor but whether one foot is in front of the other or not seems to have no significance.

(v) *Where should the typist look?* A favourite admonition is, of course, keep your eyes on the copy, and for most of the time this is correct but it should not be made into an imperial ukase. Every typist, however expert, will occasionally need to look at the typing line as a quick check on what is being produced, and also at the keys, especially when some unusual letter or character combination or figures need to be typed.

(vi) *What technique refinements should be watched for as progress is being made?* There are four refinements that develop as the learner gains in ability and confidence, and at the right moment in time these should be encouraged and referred to. They are:

(*a*) The speed of the reach and of the return to anchor position become as important as the correct fingering and choice of reach.

(*b*) When the student begins to chain common digrams and trigrams, practice material for these should be introduced (e.g. -ion, -ing, -ent, -her).

(*c*) Economy of finger and hand movement.

(*d*) The addition of automaticized skill in the other necessary manipulations with specific practice drills, viz. space bar, backspace, shift and shift-lock, carriage return, tab-key, margin release, paper handling, erasure, is also essential.

Other topics of importance in teaching typewriting of a wider application than the teaching of the keyboard now follow.

Copy

The kinds of input from which the typist may have to work are: manuscript, typescript, modified typescript, information to be recorded on forms, business documents (invoices, orders, etc.), shorthand notes, print and/or modified print, direct dictation and audio input. The last two of these involve an independent skill and training (see Chapter 7).

All the rest are in the form of some kind of copy that the typist must position most conveniently for herself. Copyholders of various types and degrees of complexity have not met with much success; they are often used in training but much less commonly in business. It is strange that this quite important matter has received such scant attention. If you have experience of typing, the answer to the question *What is the best place for the copy?* is obvious: it should be at eye level in the working position and squarely in front of the operator. Only in Pitman colleges and in one or two other schools and colleges scattered over the world have I seen a simple, sensible arrangement to meet this requirement. It has long been a source of surprise that typewriter manufacturers do not cater for this need with a simply-operated and well-engineered device forming an accessory to the machine itself to permit copy to be placed in this position.

The customary practice in training is to use copyholders placed either on the right or left of the machine at the discretion of the operator. The arguments for preferring one side or the other carry little weight and are really not relevant since neither is correct. Until typewriter manufacturers provide for these needs, the best plan may be to get a simple, stout, custom-built folding wooden stand, foolproof in use, which can be stood close behind the typewriter with a slight rake away from the vertical and adjustable in height above the working surface. It seems reasonable to assume that the present custom of laying the copy flat to one side or other of the machine and peering downwards at it must have harmful postural effects.

Fingering

The present standard fingering on the QWERTY keyboard, with negligible variation (as for example what finger to use for **B**), is accepted by all as though it were divinely decreed and inscribed on one of the tablets brought down from Sinai. I have been unable to trace either its history (except to say that in a text of 1898 it appears just as it exists now) or any research or comment on it by the many researchers in typewriting; this appears to be a topic for further research. The fingering used by the English-speaking world is not that used by some other users of the QWERTY keyboard in other languages. There is some *a priori* evidence that a typist using anchor positions on the index fingers and only six fingers and two thumbs can achieve results as fast and accurate as nine-finger touch typists.

The pattern of acquisition

In the January 1969 issue of *Industrial Engineering*, Cochran reported on a typewriting study based on the results attained by a class of 18 girls learning to type over a period of about 40 weeks. These results are tabulated and shown graphically below:

Typewriting learning data

Total output (words) produced	Rate of output (minutes/ 100 words)	Output level (words/minute)	
11,500	10·0	10·0	
20,000	9·7	10·3	
35,000	6·0	16·7	
45,000	4·7	21·3	
60,000	3·7	27·0	
80,000	3·15	31·8	
90,000	4·6	21·8	⎫ Loss of
110,000	3·6	27·8	⎬ retention after
130,000	2·9	34·4	⎭ Christmas break
170,000	2·5	40·0	
190,000	2·45	40·8	
240,000	2·4	41·7	Plateau A
260,000	2·3	43·5	
380,000	2·1	47·7	
400,000	2·8	35·8	⎫ Loss of
430,000	2·3	43·5	⎬ retention after
470,000	2·1	47·7	⎭ Easter break
500,000	2·0	50·0	
560,000	2·0	50·0	Plateau B
620,000	1·9	52·6	
680,000	1·85	54·0	
720,000	1·8	55·5	
750,000	1·7	58·5	⎫ End spurt
800,000	1·67	60·0	⎭

The curve produced is in fact typical of learning a motor skill. The progress at first is slow. Do not be deceived by the fairly quick rise in speed: it took twice as long to reach an output of 100 000 words as it did to increase that by 100 per cent to 200 000 words. Speed (and output) improvement is rapid from 30–45 wam; then the rate slows markedly and it is only in the last 'end-spurt' of a course, characteristic of seeing a goal in sight, that the curve continues with uniform, instead of decreasing, gains. Plateaux of consolidation appear at A and B when, after the sharp drops in output and speed occasioned by Christmas and Easter breaks in the programme, there is a quick recovery to D and E. Notice that improvement after about 45 wam is approximately linear.

The teaching point is that nothing will change the shape of this curve. What we can do, however, is to lift it all by 5–15 wam by improved allocation of time and teaching methods (see Speed and Accuracy Development, p. 72).

Could this curve be continued in the same linear fashion? Here we are

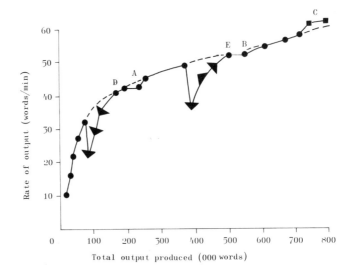

Total output produced (000 words)

in an area of doubt, and again there is a highly practical field of research open. We know that all operators must have a limited potential for further improvement; we also know that the majority of them certainly have not reached that potential. For what percentage of learners does the fact of diminishing returns operate after 60 wam, because we have not continued instruction or effective practice much beyond this point? A gifted few reach 80–100 wam. Could more of the 45-wam average typists reach these new levels if the training were continued without demands on time and training becoming intolerably high? The results of some in-service training are suggestive of a positive answer.

Errors

The first thing that needs to be said about errors in typewriting is that they are inevitable, typewriting being a field of activity in which perfection is unattainable. The second is that they are more usually random than not; the errors that can be attributed to some specific curable weakness are few. The third is that requiring learners to re-type words or practices or 'to correct their mistakes' will achieve no learning for nine-tenths of the time.

When errors are analysed they are found to fall into two general categories: technical and non-technical.

Technical errors

These are the errors that arise from faulty manipulation or key-striking technique. Some recognized types are: 'reversal' errors, i.e. correct finger motion but wrong hand, as **e** for **i**, **d** for **k**; 'substitution' errors, the most frequently occurring type, when one key is substituted for another usually adjacent to it, **s** for **a**, **r** for **e**, **v** for **b**; 'anticipation' errors in which a letter is struck earlier than needed, as in *distrub* . . . for *distrib* . . . in the word *distribution*; then there are 'dominance' errors of the kind where the typist called upon to type *sirloin* irresistibly types *sirlion* because of her chained sequence -ion. Others of similar technical origin are raised (or lowered) upper-case characters, spaces in excess or omitted, shadow characters and incorrect line spacing.

Non-technical errors

These cover a wider field but I have omitted all those that may be attributed to imperfections in shorthand notes, illegible manuscript or dubieties in an audio recording. This still leaves plenty, including those numerous instances when typists have spellings quite correct in the copy but get them wrong on the keyboard (*seperate* for *separate*, or *effect* when copy has *affect*), or any of the other mistakes that arise from inadequate linguistic knowledge. They include too the errors that arise from temporary failure of concentration as in transpositions, letters, words or lines repeated or omitted, omissions or repetitions resulting from trap cues as when a word in one line appears on another line and is accepted as the 'go-on' cue. Then there are errors attributable only to psychological quirks like *ltetres* for *letters* (it is all there but comes out in a mangled form) or the typing of a word that has intruded from the mind instead of the copy as *pornographic* for *phonographic*.

Such an analysis is only worthwhile if it enables us to prescribe some teaching practices which will help to make error less prevalent than it is.

Before attempting to do that, however, let us look at some other considerations that bear on the problem.

Personal factors enter into the question of error. It is well known that typewriting skill is subject to short-term vagaries, and performance varies from day to day and even at different times of the day. The mood and temperament of the learner, whether she feels elated or downcast, whether she has had a good night's sleep or not, has boy-friend trouble, or is being affected positively or negatively by relationships with classroom or office colleagues, will all play a part in this.

A second influence is that of *environment* and *concentration*. It has always seemed to me odd indeed that typewriting, which demands close concentration, is conducted in circumstances, whether in the class or the office, that are as inimical to this as they could very well be: noise, voices, clatter, movement, interruptions, all seem to be the natural concomitants of learning or working typists. Everything that aids concentration is going to help accuracy too.

Similarly, the right physical conditions for work—the right furniture, the good mechanical condition of the machines, the size of the working surface, the seating—all need to be right. The typist needs to be warm to be efficient; she also needs well oxygenated air and first-class lighting on the copy. Nor is the general milieu without effect: flowers, carpets, curtains, pictures, aesthetic and pleasing decor—all these may be peripheral but they add their quota to the typist's sense of well-being and contentment, and hence to her output.

Lastly, I return to the importance of reading ability, fast, close and accurate. The further one progresses in keyboard mastery, the more acute the reading problem becomes. When the learner begins she is at the wholly literal stage where each successive letter is a problem. Typing what is there is in one sense easier than it is later on when the learner has built chained responses and needs to read ahead and store mentally in readiness for conversion into the appropriate typing actions. Long words and unusual words should be mentally syllabified.

All learners can be graded into primarily vissiles, audiles and tactiles. This means that a vissile learns most efficiently what he sees, an audile what he hears and a tactile what he experiences kinaesthetically through the actual or imagined three-dimensional experience.

Fortunately, more than 80 per cent of us are primarily vissiles, but this does not mean, as we know too well from experience, that 80 per cent of us are good readers of the written word. We have to train our students to look more attentively at the words in front of them.

What emerges from this so that we can help our students towards accuracy?

(*a*) Speed forcing must be paced. Uncontrolled speed forcing will lead to a breakdown in technique and foster error (see Speed Development, p.72).

(*b*) Training copy must be clear, well-spaced, easy to see.

(*c*) Remedial drills are only effective if they relate positively to some curable defect of technique, e.g. substitution errors. Otherwise they are valueless.

(*d*) Give as much attention to correct ballistic stroking in Lesson 100 as in Lesson 1.

(*e*) Give occasional practice that demands close attention and concentration, e.g.

I hope you will be trepens at the meeting on Suetday

(*f*) Try to improve the conditions for concentration by improving the environment and working conditions.

(*g*) Give as much individual help and guidance as you can make time for.

(*h*) Give exercises in strengthening and making more flexible the fingers and hands. Even if these do not achieve much they will help to get the 'mind-set' right. Elma Whittle, a celebrated British teacher, has a range of successfully-used exercises of this type.

(*i*) Provide occasional incentives for accuracy, e.g. How far can you go before making a mistake? You will do well to get beyond two minutes. Students should be told to raise a hand when they make their first (recognized) error, but then to continue with a fresh start at that point.

Leonard West (op. cit.) has some remarks relevant to this topic: 'The suggestion of a 2-errors-per-minute standard during accuracy practice arises from the findings on average accuracy in 5-minute test timings among thousands of typing students in numerous studies, in which average number of errors has ranged between 1 and 3 centering at a little less than 2 e.p.m.

'One could, if desired, make the standards more rigorous: 3 rather than 4 errors allowed in a 2-minute practice timing, 4 or 5 rather than 6 errors allowed in a 3-minute practice timing. However, the tighter you make your accuracy standards, the more frustration students will experience; some students will be sentenced interminably to accuracy practice under such standards as 1 e.p.m. or 2 errors in 3 minutes, or 3 errors in 5 minutes. Nothing is gained by such tactics. The uselessly low reliability of straight copy error scores mandates reasonable standards of accuracy during accuracy practice, and the most useful definition of "reasonable" is that level of accuracy found to be characteristic of typists in general, namely, about 2 e.p.m.'

Erasing

Erasure in order to correct a mis-strike has been much improved in recent years by new chemical and mechanical methods, quick and handy to use. Nevertheless, there are still occasions when it is best to use typing erasers of high quality (hard and soft), a perspex backer and a soft brush. This method should be taught along with the others.

It should be taught as a drill so as to help students react immediately and naturally to an error without panic or annoyance. Until the operation becomes instinctive, erasure should be learned as a series of steps quickly executed; when it is known, the verbal cues can be discarded.

Erasing is often introduced too late; ideally it should be when necessary, during the stage when realistic work begins, probably at about 25 wam. Then it should become a regular feature in all production work to be submitted for assessment, or as required by the teacher.

Figures

Figure-character keys not unnaturally tend to get less attention than they should. They are long and difficult reaches from the home rows. On the other hand, the importance of figure work grows every year.

It is very doubtful whether it is worth the long and difficult effort to build in a pure touch skill for typing figures. The reason is that figures are always important and always have to be visually checked, since there is no telling whether a five-character number like 13709 is immediately right or wrong, unlike a five-key word like *modle* for *model* where the transposition is immediately apparent; context is no help either.

Better to allow learners not only to look (which even expert typists do) but to move their hands up as needed, provided that they return at once to the anchor positions.

Do not give drills confined to figures; always embed them in an alphabetic context in order to give the right realistic practice. From the time that the figures are taught they should continually appear in all practice material.

Practice material

The content of the practice material that we give typewriting students, whether at the keyboard-learning stage or in various production tasks, is not a matter without significance. Textbooks obviously provide much essential material, but they are never intended to be the only source of material for a particular class. How otherwise can we provide individual work, use natural interests, correlate with other subjects of the curriculum or cater for different rates of learning?

It is now accepted by the majority of teachers that at the keyboard-learning stage, meaningful sentence material is essential. At first this will be circumscribed by the students' current knowledge of the keys, but from the time when the whole keyboard is known and can be operated with a modest level of proficiency, then vocabulary should be unrestricted within the range of the students' understanding. There is no useful purpose served by giving material of low syllabic intensity or limited to common words; students, as we have seen, do not learn to type by words.

Content at this stage can serve the dual purpose of providing useful information or interesting matter on a wide range of subjects, paragraphs of literary merit included. Of the first kind we might have a short paragraph (including figures) about NCR paper; of the second, a descriptive passage like that of the feast of broiled lamb in Lawrence's *Revolt in the Desert*.

Clearly, when production work is being done the content must generally have a business bias and use a business vocabulary. But it should at least be in an acceptable, informal style free from jargon, technicalities or grammatical mistakes; it should be up-to-date and reasonably topical and realistic.

Pacing

Speed forcing is a part of skill-building; we must push the students for speed otherwise their progress will be unnecessarily slow. The trouble is that pressure for speed is always associated with a rise in the error rate. The solution to this lies first in separating speed practice from accuracy practice and, secondly, in controlling the speed forcing by pacing.

In the very early stages the pacing comes first from the teacher calling the strokes and then from the student pacing herself. In a little while when the student is able to type for a minute continuously without undue strain, we can pace by calling the quarter minutes, or by using a timing tape if we have the typewriting room audio-equipped, or a 'pinger' clock. Then the students have a goal to aim at, and if ahead of time they know they should slow down a little so as to arrive at the next quarter-minute at exactly the right time. Here, for example, is a one-minute pacing drill at 25 wam; that is, it contains 125 strokes on a 50-stroke line, each quarter-minute being marked by a superior dot.

For many years the USA comprised only 48 states but today there are 50, Hawaii and Alaska being the most recent newcomers.

Drills like this should be used regularly all through the typewriting course, and applied so that the controlled speed forcing is alternated with practice without any speed requirement, only accuracy.

Speed and accuracy development

The topic now to be examined from the teaching viewpoint is one that has always been, and still remains, controversial. There is a general (but not unanimous) agreement today that sight-typing is necessary in the early stages, that speed forcing must be used in keyboard training, that the avoidance of error is the correct approach rather than the correction of error (except where it can clearly be seen to arise from faulty technique). It is also generally agreed, as we shall see when we look at production typewriting more specifically, that the pressure of time must still be sustained in all the varied jobs in which students must gain realistic experience. It is here that divergence of views begins: should plain copy typing be maintained as a permanent feature of a typewriting course? If it is, how can we cater for the individual differences in ability that inevitably develop sufficiently to be a problem fairly early in a course? How can valuable practice be economically given both for raising speed and accuracy?

First, there is the point that straight line-by-line copying is unrealistic as typists are seldom called upon to do it in their jobs. Second, research in the USA shows that at least straight-copy skill is not transferred to job-tasks as much as might be supposed. Third, there is the point that what we call production typing is unquestionably the real objective of all typewriting training outside the sphere of personal typing.

The case will be found forcefully presented in Leonard West (op. cit. Chapter 13). On two points, the author deferentially endorses the work of the master: (i) 'Specifically ordinary copying speed as measured in straight-copy tests shows quite good relationships with production speed, whereas straight-copy accuracy or quality of production work does not'; (ii) 'That a 40 wam copyist will more rapidly acquire production skill than a 25 wam copyist is true but beside the point'—but is it really 'beside the point'?— 'Planning factors so thoroughly swamp stroking factors in production skill that no choice exists but to start production typing early.'

Production typing of quality is unquestionably the goal. Nevertheless, the speed-stroking component and the accuracy component are always present. It pays to give some attention after the first 35–45 periods, if not in every subsequent period then at least in every alternate one, to these; this need not occupy more than 10–15 minutes as we shall try to show. Isolating these two components so that the student has nothing to concentrate on except the single goal of controlled speed forcing or the controlled accuracy, with all irrelevancies (from this viewpoint) such as 'Where do I type what?' and 'How do I divide at this line end?' removed from the practice, serves a valuable purpose. Employers still expect typists to be able to prove their copy speeds as well as give evidence of their qualifications in the field of production typewriting. The author does not believe that they are wholly wrong.

There is a way to give this kind of practice in an efficient and economical way. The difficulty in the past has been to cater for individual aims and yet remain in the group situation with the benefits that derive from all working together for a common end.

A whole range of passages is prepared giving precisely measured practice at speeds from 20 wam upwards in steps of one word a minute and arranged so that the students can work on one-, two-, three- or four-minute pieces. The passages themselves contain figures and the full range of characters on the keyboard and they are self-contained pieces of interest and value in themselves. Then each student can be slotted into the appropriate speed level and aim first to secure an advance of three or four minutes disregarding errors other than skill-breakdown errors like moving on to the wrong bank of the machine. The aim is then changed and the student covers the same ground to consolidate the rise in speed on an error-tolerance scale which permits the slower student a higher percentage of errors than the more able student.

Practice of this kind, when properly conducted, achieves the aims of raising the speed and reducing the errors—or at least of keeping them within a constant percentage level, and from the students' viewpoint it is interesting, challenging and motivating work which they engage in enthusiastically.*

Production typewriting

The term 'production typing' is now generally accepted and understood

* See *Raise the Speed: Reduce the Errors,* Canning (Pitman), in which a course of the kind described is presented with the method and all the necessary materials for carrying it out. The statements made in the text above are based on validation, the evidence of which is repeated in the Preface to the book.

to mean all typing activities that are of the kind the typist may be called upon to perform in the actual work situation. Its main constituents are non-typing activities as well as those keyboard and manipulative duties that are required to be applied to any specialized task. In the non-typing activities are included the acquisition of knowledge of the accepted conventions to be observed, knowing where to put what, and then—most important of all—the planning and decisions that have to be taken to get the material correctly displayed on the page. These are decisions about line length, margins, tabulation, use of space, size of paper, placement in relation to head, foot and margins, display for maximum legibility and ease of understanding.

Good textbooks provide all the knowledge, all the kinds of production typewriting and guidance about all the decisions that have to be taken. Their weaknesses in the past have been first that they have tended to spoonfeed the students with full and exhaustive information about every kind of exercise, and give them far too little experience in working on a set job-task without guidance. The student can only learn by doing and must in the last resort make all the decisions for herself; the sooner we can get the student relying on herself the better. A second weakness has been that large amounts of unnecessary typing have been incorporated. If a student is learning where to put the various parts of a simple sort of business leter and, given a particular length, how to make the decisions of the kind described above so as to set the letter correctly on the sheet (and what sheet to set it on), then the requirement of typing 200 words in the body of the letter is an irrelevance. Exercises have been too long; they need to be much shorter and concentrated more exclusively on the goal of the particular learning and practice that is going on.

It is obvious that maximum transfer will take place when the tasks the student learns and practises are exactly those that the office will demand. What are these tasks? It is time that we kept ourselves better informed of this by research into the gradually changing pattern of these. The author's own limited survey, several years ago, showed in an undiscriminating way that typists were called upon to devote, 30 per cent of their typing time to manuscript, 44 per cent to letters, memorandums and reports, and the remainder to a wide variety of different jobs. Some of these were: envelopes, form-filling, invoices and other specific printed business documents, pro formas, notices, programmes, itineraries, schedules of work, statistical tables, lists, minutes, agenda, stencil and offset masters (very few spirit masters), indexes and cards for filing systems. In addition to these there are many more specialized tasks like computer input, technical data, specifications, wills, conveyances and legal documents generally, scripts for radio and TV, scenarios, typescript manuscripts for printing, originals for camera and litho-printing, foreign-language typing and the like. Since the range and difficulty of typing tasks is great enough already, it seems unnecessary, except in specialized courses or for the requirements of examination syllabuses, to include such specialist work.

The questions we now have to consider are: When should production typewriting begin? What should we begin with? And what to continue with? What principles should be followed in teaching and in practice exercises? What methods may be used?

It is not really practicable or efficient to begin production work until students have a reasonable competence on the keyboard of about 25 wam. Before this, too much of their time and attention will be diverted to the problems of keyboard operating. On the other hand, it is important to get on to these tasks quickly, first because they are the real goal of the learning process and secondly because the variety of typing applications to be covered and knowledge to be acquired is considerable. So, in short, we begin as soon as is practicable.

It seems reasonable to start with the very simple kind of business letter, and to use simplified block layout from the beginning, which is steadily becoming more widely acceptable, especially since its adoption by government departments as a result of the sponsorship of the Civil Service Department. Briefly, the system is that all document details are typed to one left-hand margin; they may be distinguished from one another or arranged in hierarchical order by the use of white space, un-spaced upper-case letters for headings and titles and initially-capitalized words underscored for further sub-headings. Outside the 'body' of the letter or document, no punctuation is required. Line-end divisions are avoided if possible, as are centrings, roman numerals and display features.

This layout can be applied to letters, memorandums, reports, menus, notices, envelopes—indeed most typewritten documents including columnar work where the tab-stops can operate as a series of 'left-hand' margins, internal centring being ignored.

The layout has acquired its rising popularity because of its simplicity and the important 8–10 per cent saving in time that its use brings. Not unnaturally the typist, once introduced to it, is reluctant to use any other method. Its appearance strikes some people as unpleasing but it is clear, neat, simple and legible. For complete details the reader is referred to the two articles that appeared in *Office Skills* (May/June 1973) and to *Industrial and Commercial Training* (January 1975).

Now there are two ways open to the teacher. Either the course can progress step by step from very simple, short business letters through to

Capital	Country	Round Trip Air Fare
		£
Paris	France	45
Washington	USA	176
Athens	Greece	84
Tehran	Iran	140
Canberra	Australia	261

SIMPLIFIED BLOCK

Capital	Country	Round Trip Air Fare
		£
Paris	France	45
Washington	USA	176
Athens	Greece	84
Tehran	Iran	140
Canberra	Australia	261

CENTRED DISPLAY

The simplified block has a 30 per cent advantage in time.

long letters with continuation sheets, titles, references, circulated copy
details, signatory's official designation and internal tabulation, and thus
exhaustively cover one very common and important job-task; or several
of these broad topics—manuscript, tables, displayed material, minutes
etc.—can be started within a few days and then carried forward step by
step on successive days. This cyclic method has the advantage of maintaining interest and motivation, and lends itself also to the small-step
principle. There is nothing that requires us, for example, to teach
everything about a letter, even a simple one, in a single session. With

many students it may be better to teach only two or three items—the date, the reference line and the inside address—and to give four or five exercises on these by dividing plain A5 and A4 sheets into two or three by rulings and using each of these as a letterhead.

In each succeeding lesson, cover the points already learned by brief comment, using a model, but concentrate the instruction on the new points to be introduced. Cut out all irrelevancies: for example, if the points to be covered are the subscription, the signatory's name, designation and copy and enclosure details in a letter, then there is no need to type a body to the letter of 100 words or more, the last two lines will be sufficient. After appropriate practice, of course, it will be necessary to 'put it all together' in a complete exercise, but not until the specific practice has been satisfactorily performed and the students are confident what to do.

It is a fact that little or no validated research has yet been done into teaching methods for production typewriting. We must therefore rely on our general principles of time-skills teaching to guide us. One successful method is to begin by using a correct model from a textbook, and if this can be shown by means of an OHP colour transparency that is the best way, since then the teacher can show the class what to notice by direct indication. Then the students work through an example with some guidance. The next stage is for the students to go on to similar exercises but this time they are left to make their own decisions. The completed exercises are then compared with correct versions, once again from a textbook or by OHP transparency. A different method is by verbal instruction, the students typing the material dictated at a smart pace on successive directions from the teacher with comments en route. When the procedure has been repeated on one or two further examples, the students are then given fresh material and once again left to draw the conclusions from their guided practice and apply them on their own to the given material. This 'on your own' approach is important.

At this point it may be pointed out that long and complex instructions on counting for centring and display are, in the office situation, seldom applied, either because the necessity for them is avoided by using simplified block layout or because the typist has learned to use the judgement of her eye combined with the minimum amount of centring (e.g. longest line). At some stage in training such judgements should be encouraged and tried out.

It is just as important in production typewriting to apply the pressure of time as it is in straight keyboard work. Most production work should demand a sense of urgency and modern textbooks acknowledge this by indicating 'standard times' for the assignments. What the standard time ought to be must, however, depend on the ability and aptitude of the typist. Here, as in all time-skills, we have to cope with the problem of individual differences.

Two basic ways of doing this are available. We can work on the principles:

(*a*) How long did it take you to complete this task?
(*b*) How much of this task can you get done in *x* minutes?

Both ways should be used.

It also helps to assign three timings for a task or sequence of short tasks: slow (set deliberately long to encourage the less able who will manage to beat it), standard, and fast time.

It will be necessary to emphasize the need for fast, concentrated work all through job-tasks and to keep this goal in the forefront of the students' minds by maintaining and publishing the timings achieved. This need for bursts of concentration with a serious effort to step up the pace is a further argument in favour of numerous short and specific exercises rather than fewer but long ones. Longer exercises are not of value until the later stages of a course (100 hours or more) when students have confidence and reasonable ability over a range of production tasks and have begun to build up the typing stamina that they will need in the work situation.

At about this time, too, linked sequences of exercises will begin to be of value, first because they give a fresh interest to the work and, second, because they cover a range of typing activity. Here are some examples:

Committee-work sequence
 Copy terms of reference and constitution of the committee.
 Letter to convene the committee.
 Agenda.
 Minutes.
 Short financial statement.
 A Chairman's agenda.

Arranging a meeting
 Writing to speakers.
 Speakers' replies.
 Booking accommodation and catering.
 Circular on subject of meeting to members.
 Notices to be posted.
 Report for the press.
 Paragraph in secretary's report to committee.

Going on a business trip
  MS notes from executive about the trip.
  Letter to travel agent confirming telephone conversation.
  Reply from agent with some modifications.
  Letter of acceptance.
  Itinerary.
  Letters to two overseas agents notifying of arrival.

(There is an excellent textbook for such sequences—*Ten Topics for Typists*, Pat Brady (Pitman).)

Display principles

The teacher has to ensure that students understand the purpose of displaying material. The only one that really matters is that the information shall be conveyed to the reader in the most immediately effective and readable way. The questions to be asked are: Which are the important items? How are they related? What is the real purpose of the document?

There are really no rules about displaying material beyond satisfying these requirements. It is true that many large business organizations lay down a house-style which they expect all their employees to follow. Sometimes this style gives rules for almost every conceivable type of document circulating within the business but more often it concerns itself only with letters, memorandums and reports.

Simple blocked display with appropriate use of white space, capital letters and underscoring will often achieve a result in every way as legible and generally comprehensible as a much more elaborate style on which three times as much time (and therefore money) has been expended.

The simpler, economical means of displaying material where judgement and planning play a more important part than complex calculations is rightly becoming more and more acceptable.

Tabulation principles

It has already been pointed out that in some forms of tabulated material at least the block principle will serve just as effectively as in a letter or a notice. In more complicated tables where calculation is regarded as essential, then the vital point is where to start each heading and each column both vertically and horizontally.

Use of chalkboard diagrams (kept simple) and/or OHP transparencies in two colours are essential when tabular work is being taught. If, as is usual, the material can be displayed with an equal number of spaces for the margins and between the columns, the easy method is:

(*a*) number of type spaces required;
(*b*) deduct from 80 (pica) or 96 (elite);
(*c*) divide remainder by number of blank spaces required.

When some different arrangement is called for because of the peculiarities of the document or the material, then the inter-column spaces must be separately decided and aggregated, either before or after margins have been decided upon.

Marking, assessment, examinations, checking and correcting

Marking typing papers and assessing attainment are dealt with in the separate chapter on this subject. Checking and correcting, which are of obvious importance in typewriting, is dealt with in Chapter 8 on Transcription.

6 Teaching Shorthand

The teaching task: defining aims and objectives

A teacher setting out to teach shorthand to a class of students starts out with some initial advantages and some special problems that will have to be solved. The initial advantages are the interest and the keenness of the students to learn the subject, which arise out of its relevance to their vocational needs which they realize, and also out of its complete novelty and the challenge that it presents. Furthermore, all the students begin 'at scratch', knowing nothing at all of the subject. The special problems that the teacher faces will be briefly described in the next section. None of them are insoluble; how difficult they are will often depend upon the general level of educational attainment of the individuals in the class and primarily their grasp of their own language since this skill, like all the others discussed in this book, can only work through the medium of language.

Since the overall aim of teaching shorthand is the highly practical one of bringing the students to the point where they confidently write it correctly at speeds from three to six or more times faster than ordinary longhand and equally confidently read their own shorthand and transcribe it into the conventional form with accuracy and speed, it is most important for the teacher to have clearly in mind the separate aim and objective of each activity that forms a part of the overall process. So we should ask ourselves continually: What contribution is this making to the ultimate goal? What benefit do I expect the students to gain from this? Is the method I am using the best for student learning? Is it best for these particular students? This means that the accomplished teacher will command methods and materials, while remaining sensitive to the special individual and class needs, so that both may be varied to achieve the best result.

All this involves the process of selection that is at the core of good teaching; no teaching situation is static and no two classes are identical. Some methods are used successfully by some teachers but not by others; some students react favourably, others unfavourably.

The point is made, therefore, that the discussions that follow describe methods, materials and activities that the author or other teachers have found effective and are directly and consciously related to those general principles of skill-teaching already described.

Initial problems of students

Some of the special problems of skills-teaching generally have already been considered in Chapter 4 and they should, if necessary, be referred to again at this point.

In this chapter, we concern ourselves exclusively with Pitman's Shorthand, and in particular with Pitman 2000, although almost everything that is said will have an equal relevance to New Era Shorthand.

Shorthand is a wholly symbolic and very largely phonetic form of writing. Students will have to know, therefore, the differences between a consonant, a vowel, a diphthong and a diphone (double vowel), and be able to recognize them at once. Furthermore, they will need to discriminate between the sounds of the English vowels, as between those in *boot* and *book* or *law* and *lore*, and between the consonants as in *prestige* and *ridge*. Such knowledge cannot be assumed; however, with some regular practice in the early stages, most students will soon become sound-conscious in a way they never had been previously.

If they are to write shorthand they will have to accept a speed of action in writing that may at first give them trouble. Here again, if the standard is set early on, as it must be, and persisted in, students will quickly get used to it and come to accept it. As in the stroking technique for typewriting, writing a shorthand outline at 20 wam is quite different in nature from writing the same outline at 100 or more wam. It is towards the second goal that we must aim right from the start.

Students will also need to accept the discipline of periods of intense effort and serious concentration to acquire the skill. Sometimes students who have had the greatest part of their education in academic and intellectual activity will find this irksome, but generally the enthusiasm and persistence of the teacher will carry them through this stage without serious difficulty.

Since shorthand is but one more manifestation of language, the students' command of it must play a part in the shorthand-learning process. In particular, the range of their vocabulary and their more explicit understanding of basic sentence structures is going to help them. We have no time in our shorthand course to give specific instruction in these matters, but no opportunity should be lost of incidental teaching and reminders as the occasion requires. If the class is concurrently following an English course of the limited and special type suggested by the English for Office Skills examination of Pitman Examination Institute, this will prove of the greatest value to them.*

Classroom organization, equipment and teaching aids

Fortunately, the demands made by shorthand on classroom arrangement and equipment are modest: a chair, a firm plain surface at the right height for writing, a good notebook, a good pen and good textbook are the basic needs.

The students' positions must, however, be arranged so that the teacher can circulate easily at all times, since supervised practice is essential, and it will very frequently be necessary to watch individual students at work.

By a 'good' notebook is meant one with a smooth paper surface that helps rather than hinders the pen. It should be fairly thin, not requiring the hand to be raised uncomfortably above the writing surface, containing a five-inch line of writing, this being known by long experience to be the correct length for economical hand and forearm movement. It should be specially bound—or, at least, one that lies perfectly flat when opened with no disposition for the pages to rise of their own volition—with a page length of about eight inches, this being the optimum length that will obviate actual body movements to accommodate to a longer page.

By a 'good' pen is meant one that has sufficient 'body' to be comfortably held, and writes a fine, fluent line, is readily flexible in use and maintains an even and continuous flow of ink. †

Pencils are often used but there is no doubt of the superiority of a pen. Pencils are too thin, their points break and the writing line does not remain consistent.

The following items of equipment are desirable in a room where shorthand is to be taught, over and above the basic furniture:

(1) Roller-type chalkboard with a perfectly matt green or black surface and/or a tear-off plain white 3 × 2 ft pad.

(2) A stop-clock and/or a pinger clock.

(3) Large display board.

---

* See also *Transcription Training* Canning (Pitman), and Chapter 8 below.

† Such a pen is the Senator, available directly from Pitman.

(4) Audio installation providing one-channel output to all student places and/or a multi-channel installation with student channel selection and/or individual cassette playbacks.

(5) A supply of *Pitman's Dictionary* (1974) and/or *First Dictionary*. Students should be encouraged to buy their own.

(6) A store cupboard for notebooks, paper, sets of *Memo*, of *2000* and stationery.

(7) A bookcase of general reference books.

(8) An OHP or *Diopta* for giving shorthand reading practice etc.

Most teachers nowadays have the facility of some type of audio aid. It is likely that cassette playbacks and video-tape will also become more widely used.

Cassette playbacks with earpieces enable the teacher to give individual students help of a specialist kind and may play their part as a general class-teaching aid in speed development, each student being provided with a battery-operated playback with separate earpieces and the appropriate cassettes.

Video-tape will provide substitute or supplementary teaching in situations where at any time there is a temporary shortage of teachers, or for some specific purposes (e.g. explaining and demonstrating the theory).

Teaching approach

In order to acquire the skill of shorthand it is necessary to learn a corpus of knowledge—the 'rules', principles and arbitraries that constitute the system. Once these are thoroughly learned and understood they can be applied and the outlines for a large number of common words automaticized until the superstructure of theory, like the scaffolding when a building is erected, is no longer necessary, except when the building needs renovation or repair. Only rarely does the expert writer have to refer back to rule—yet without rule the system could not exist.

There is often controversy about the order in which this corpus of essential knowledge should be presented. For example, it is agreed that since S is indispensable for plurals and third-person present tense of verbs, then the small circle should be taught very early. Again, it is argued that concentration on straight strokes only at the start is distorting in its effect on penmanship; and again, that in order to permit reasonably sophisticated and meaningful material to be presented to the students quite early on, the 69 words that represent 50 per cent of all

English material should be learned in the first half-dozen lessons. In Pitman 2000 account has been taken of these arguments.

The risk is that in presenting this indispensable material to students the teacher will say too much, take too long, teach more than is necessary and allow too little time for the vital student activities: the teacher will be too active and the learners too passive. In such a situation, the skill learning is at a minimum.

Therefore we can say that as a general guide, teacher presentation should not take longer than five minutes at a time in any one period without demands being made on the students, and that two such periods of presentation in one learning session of 40–60 minutes are about the maximum permissible. Economy of words, effectiveness of method, selection of what to use as base material—in short, planning—therefore become very important. Out of the approach, the methods and activities will spring.

A *reading approach* is widely favoured and for good reasons. If shorthand is to be learned, we must surround the student with correct specimens so that they may be absorbed. Even after the ideal presentation, it will only be the best students who can excogitate the right outlines and read the continuous and meaningful context in which they are embedded before they go on to write them; and when they write them, they must be reading them at the same time. This is why the exercise that requires transliteration from longhand into shorthand is only occasionally introduced, more to bring in the re-motivating element of variety than for any other reason. It is also the main reason why most modern shorthand texts contain the maximum amount of written shorthand and the minimum of explanatory text. Much of the actual writing of shorthand in the reading approach is done while the text is actually being read or dictated. The basic idea is the sound principle of excluding the risk of error as far as possible.

Shorthand is not a puzzle-solving activity. For this reason, the conventional alphabetic symbols for the shorthand of the presentation should be available to the student and in Pitman 2000 this practice has been followed. It is also an argument in favour of providing individual students with dictation practice as the key to the work they will do in the *Pitman 2000 Workbook* (Paris 1 and 2).

A *functional approach* is one in which the concentration is not on the rules or the understanding of the intellectual principles behind them but on a more or less empirical presentation of the outlines. It might be expressed as familiarity first, assimilation and understanding afterwards. Carried to its logical extreme, shorthand might be presented as ordinary longhand print (letterpress) with the introduction of a gradually increasing number of words. The choice of the words to be introduced step by step would in the first place be made according to frequency: since we know that 69 words represent 50 per cent of all average English matter, it would seem sensible to begin with these, most of them being arbitraries. Then we would introduce classes of words, e.g. final circle **S** words with straight strokes and curves in contexts where a high inevitability of transcript was a factor. Theoretically at least, it would be possible to carry the principle all the way through the shorthand learning, although nobody to the author's knowledge has yet done this. Nevertheless, the functional approach is a suggestive one. Students need not be expected to apply rules on new material, or in the early stages of learning to construct new outlines. The mind is concentrated on reading and later on writing outlines in context and, to a much slighter extent, on the rules. There are very few rules in shorthand that need to be learned by heart and none that should be copied out. All the concentration should be on the actual shorthand. It is this concentration that is the core of the functional approach.

The inductive (discovery) principle of learning has already been discussed earlier. From the particular the students learn the generalization that applies by working it out for themselves. To give only a single illustration of an idea which is generally easy enough to apply to any area of learning the shorthand theory—if we write on the chalkboard and simultaneously read to the students:

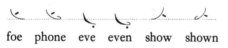

foe   phone   eve   even   show   shown

we can then expect them to read

know   ?   my   ?   low   ?

and then deduce the general rule from these examples.

The opposite and more commonly used approach is to state a rule, giving examples, and then expect the student to be able first to read and then to write further examples of the same rule presented to them. This is the *deductive or 'telling' approach.* For example, we might say while presenting the outlines, 'If **R** begins a word it is generally written upward as in these words:

road   rate   ripe   rig   reach

but if **R** begins a word and a vowel comes before it, then we write **R** downward, as in these words:

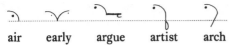

air　　early　　argue　　artist　　arch

Then this learning step can be consolidated by using the *question and answer* approach. We can say: 'Now tell me why the **R** is upward in this word:

rich?'

and when we have elicited a precise statement, go on to ask: 'And why is the **R** downward in this word:

ark?'

It will not be enough to accept the spontaneous answer that is almost sure to come: 'Because there is a vowel in front of the **R**.' It is equally important to elicit the second part of the statement '. . . and because **R** is the first consonant in the word' or '. . . because **R** begins the word'. The *question and answer approach* has several advantages if it is kept brisk and short, and as many of the students as possible contribute an answer; they begin to understand the practical application of the rule, and then it is easy to ask 'Why? What is the point of such a rule?' They are being required to think and to sharpen and clarify their understanding. From this approach also, it will be easy to identify the students who have mastered the idea and those who are having some difficulty.

Each of these approaches is *a* way, but not *the* way. All of them can be used according to the judgement of the teacher, and each can be used in combination with any other. Their success will depend on the command and expertise of the teacher.

Penmanship: writing shorthand

In every shorthand lesson, specific attention will need to be given to the way students write it. Transfer from the fluency and legibility of ordinary handwriting seems not to be very significant. Symbolic writing at speed is a separate skill resting on manual and digital dexterity, and delicacy and refinement of movement. The quality and speed of this writing will play a highly significant part in the overall success of the student as a shorthand writer (and reader). Specific training in writing by demonstration, instruction and drill is necessary all the way through the learning process up to speeds of 100 wam or more, but most particularly in the first 50 or 60 periods of the course. The essential elements on which concentration must be directed are:

(a) Lightness of touch
Shorthand writing can hardly be too light; it can very easily be too heavy. Lightness is a factor in both speed and stamina, and students have to understand this from the start. Almost without exception, students accustomed to their own handwriting habits will write shorthand too heavily, too ponderously and too slowly at first. The way to achieve lightness is a very relaxed hold on the pen so that the grip of the fingers is only just sufficient to keep it in place and a conscious relaxation of the whole forearm to the elbow. Students should be taught that no shorthand strokes are heavy; they are to be distinguished as light and very light. The author has had success in this by teaching them the distinction between the so-called 'light and heavy' or 'light and dark' or 'thin and thick' strokes (all these descriptions are unsatisfactory) by presenting the so-called heavy part of the pair, e.g. **V** before **F**, **B** before **P** and so on, and then reversing the usual process of saying: 'You write **B** a little more heavily than **P**' by saying: '**B** is light but **P** is still lighter.'

Unless students acquire lightness of touch, they are certain to be hindered when they seek to build their speed. It helps to show on the display board a specimen of your ordinary handwriting and below it your shorthand: the contrast in density of line should be immediately apparent.

(b) Speed and cursiveness of execution
It is only natural that when students begin to write what is to them at first as unfamiliar as Celtic runes, they should be slow, cautious and cumbersome. We have to insist at once that, even if mistakes are made, the writing must be fast (at least 50 wam) and fluent. Demonstrate on the chalkboard the difference there is between 'copperplate' outlines and quick 'flick' outlines. They appear different and their execution is even more markedly so. When correct shorthand is being copied, demand it at an initial speed of 50 wam and ensure that they keep up this pace; show them repeatedly how easy this really is if it is kept light and the pen is moved smoothly over the paper in a relaxed but delicately controlled way. In the early stages we have plenty of two- or three-stroke

outlines and the short forms and phrases to work on. Show the students
how in writing a word like

package

the pauses between **P** and **K**, and **K** and **J**, are infinitesimal. Write the
whole outline at one go, not one stroke and then another.

Naturally, this requirement will take time, but persist. Tell the
students to concentrate at first on only two things—keeping up the pace
and writing lightly; the other requirements will soon follow. In the section below on *Student Activities* there are several specifically concerned
with penmanship.

(*c*) *Size: uniformity of size; distinction of size*
Students will write shorthand in the size that comes naturally to them.
We ought to allow this, provided that the style adopted is not too
exaggeratedly large with only about four or five outlines per notebook
line, or so small as to pose real problems of legibility. On a 4-in. writing
line, which is the notebook standard (with an additional 1-in. margin),
about ten to twelve outlines is recommended as being the most legible
and economical in terms of movement.

Students will often write outlines and strokes that are not uniform in
size. For instance, **M** and **N** will often be written shorter than, say, **T** or
D, and straight downstrokes will often be longer than straight up-
strokes. Such faults must be watched for and corrected.

When style is to be distinguished, there is no harm in a little
exaggeration provided that joining strokes are not thereby distorted.
For example, **SHUN** hook, **SES** circle and **-STER** may be larger than
they appear in copperplate, and so may **KW**; doubling can be swift and
bold; halving quite unmistakably halved compared with normal length
strokes, and so on. The risk is that in writing, say, a **SES** to an **F** in
faces , the size of the circle may tend to increase the size of the
stroke; the same is true when writing -**SHUN** or -**STER** to curves or
straight strokes.

(*d*) *Correctness of formation*
When strokes or modifications of strokes are first encountered, it is
worthwhile to demonstrate these on the chalkboard in a 'larger-than-
life' form (10 or 12 in. long for a stroke, for example) and then again
later, when the students are engaged in writing, actually show them how

by writing in their notebooks. The main points that are found to need attention are these:

(1) Circle **S** must be kept small, round and complete to its stroke.

(2) All the **R-L** and **N-F (V)** series must be small, semi-circular and open to the stroke—not angled and not bent in towards the stroke.

(3) **F, V, L, R** down, **SH, ZH** must be full-bodied quarter circles; **M, N, NG, TH, S** shallow 'watchglass' curves.

(4) Strokes that are both initially and finally hooked must be kept straight.

In practice, once symbolic writing has become familiar along the lines suggested, there is no manual or digital problem in writing shorthand at any speed up to well above 100 wam; only then does dexterity and digital skill become an important factor. Writing the 4–6 per cent extra that Pitman 2000 demands, for example, is no problem at all up to 120 or 130 wam. It will be found in almost all cases that the problem is one of the mind and not one of the hand.

Theory

(*a*) Most people see a natural division between the theory stage, when the students are learning the complete system so as to be able to cope with any word in the language, and the speed-development stage, when they are raising the speed at which they can read and write shorthand, and steadily extending their automatic vocabulary. This is reasonable provided that it is recognized that the two have an area of total overlap. Speed development begins in the first lesson; theoretical perfection remains a goal all the way up the scale to 200 wam or beyond. The pressure of time operates equally in the field of theory, just as the need for the extension and perfection of theoretical knowledge operates in the field of speed.

A number of statements have already been made about teaching the student the elements of the system. We must now look more closely at this stage in the learning.

(*b*) The teacher has first to consider how much in terms of subject matter ought to be presented in one teaching unit. In a subject like shorthand, where much of the basic knowledge has to be used automatically and brought to the stage of over-learning, practice of one kind or another must dominate the unit. It is obvious that the amount of new knowledge that can be presented will be less than in a descriptive or academic subject. Textbooks are not a guide to the solution of this problem; they are never intended as method books. The order and the manner of presentation is a matter for selection and judgement according to the known needs and capabilities of the students. Often what appears as an entity in the textbook will need to be broken down into separate steps if the students are to learn efficiently. This means that supplementary material, perhaps only of a temporary kind, will need to be prepared; this will, however, be a saving in correction and remedial work. With experience, the teacher will collect some material which can be used over a quite long period with different classes, either because it meets a recurring need or because it has an intrinsic value not in the textbook. The principle of graduated units of work and practice accords with those principles of teaching skills that have already been considered.

In a general way it can be said that not more than a fifth of the available unit time should be used in successive steps of presentation. The rest must be devoted to the essential practice through a variety of student activities later to be described.

(c) A further question will have to be answered. How quickly are we to attempt to cover all the theory? With students of good ability, a fairly short period of time (six or seven weeks in terms of lapsed time, and 40–60 periods in terms of teaching units) may be advantageous; we are thinking here in terms of Pitman 2000. Students will be brought more swiftly to see the wood, instead of being lost among the trees. Their overall view of the system can be consolidated and revised concurrently with speed-development work, and a different kind of theory textbook, not constricted by the need to avoid anticipation of theoretical knowledge, will provide the student with an enhanced and enlarged view of the system.

At other times, when working with less able groups, the teacher may prefer to present small units of theory thoroughly practised before moving on. However, one should consider that if too long is spent on this stage, the students may begin to lose heart and inwardly question their ability to master the whole system.

Harm Harms of Columbus University, Ohio, wrote in 1940 (*Methods in Vocational Business Education*, South Western Publishing Co., Cincinnati), 'Sufficient evidence is now on record to warrant the statement that new words should be introduced in contextual (sentence or paragraph) form in order to secure the most efficient learning. This means that word lists and drills on individual words should be used sparingly.'

True enough—and although we are more or less bound to introduce individual word examples when presenting new theory, it is not always necessary to use all the words given. In any case we should move on quickly to the contextual practice.

(*d*) Into our teaching unit we have to incorporate the following necessary elements: new presentation linked, if that is appropriate, to previous knowledge; practice on the new presentation; reading shorthand; copying shorthand; learning and practising the short forms; learning and practising phrasing principles; copied dictation; penmanship exercises; timed dictation on known material; 'free' dictation on unprepared material (but not requiring new vocabulary); revision of knowledge to date.

Clearly, it will not always be possible to include each of these in every unit of teaching, but none must be neglected for longer than a period or two, and some will be indispensable. Apart from the presentation of new material already discussed, each of these topics needs to be looked at more closely from the viewpoint of its necessity and value, and of its possible methods of application. It will also become clear that a good deal of what is discussed will also be relevant when we come to think about the speed-development stage.

Reading shorthand

It is not in doubt that constant shorthand reading has a considerable relevance to writing ability. Students must be encouraged to read shorthand at every spare moment: it will come hard to them at first but, with persistence, will become easier.

In the theory stage, we want our students to read all the textbook material and we can add our own pieces and passages from *2000* or *Memo* (the weekly magazines for office-skills students and workers) at the appropriate level. Once all the theory is mastered then our students can turn to read anything written in shorthand; there is a weekly supply of varied material in the magazines. For Pitman 2000, we have *Dictation Practice,* its *Workbook* (Parts I and II) and the audio presentation to assist us.

It is rarely sufficient to read a piece once. If our goal is fluency and speed with the ultimate and unattainable goal of reading ability in shorthand equal to that of ordinary print, and if we also use reading as we ought—as a means of increasing knowledge of, and familiarity with, word outlines and phrases—their repetition is essential.

A variety of techniques is available:

(1) If a textbook exercise is being read for the first time then it is a time-saving device if the teacher reads the piece first (not more than

about 100 words at a time) at a comfortable rate, the students following the shorthand closely; how closely they are following will need to be checked from time to time. Then the students read a line or a sentence each when named to do so. There is no prescription that a whole text-book exercise must be done at one time; it will often be more advantageous for part of an exercise to be tackled in this way, and then used for other necessary activities. Alternatively, the reading may be prepared by the student using the keys provided in *Pitman 2000 First Course*.

In this type of reading, as in all others, a problem will recur from time to time: the individual student will 'get stuck'. Now it may help the student's learning considerably to ponder the outline and systematically work it out. But the kinds of activities we are describing here are teaching and learning activities, and not test activities. Therefore give the student the word(s) at once; prompt immediately the student falters, or allow another student to do so. If a student is particularly weak, then it is clear that she has not been concentrating or has not done the preparation required. Such students must be required to re-read the passage when the sentence ends. We cannot afford to hold up the work of twenty or more individuals, even for a few seconds, for the sake of one. All reading must be done at the smartest pace possible; indeed, as we shall later describe in this section, sometimes a prescribed reading rate must be required of the students.

(2) When well managed, the 'outline' technique keeps the whole group on the qui vive and is a lively reading method for a three- or four-minute spell. Students take it in turns in an agreed order to read one outline only; the next student reads the following one, and so on. The teacher every now and then interposes an outline so that students do not ignore what is happening in order to get ready for 'their own'. If a student falters pass straight on to the next and the next until the right response comes.

(3) Two students may read together. The weaker student is the reader, and the more able student is the prompter. Do not keep the same pairs for very long or emotive problems may arise.

(4) Reading from chalkboard shorthand has the advantage of concentrating the attention of the whole class on to one point, and it is a useful method when the teacher, who should use a pointer, wishes to comment on the outlines. It must not be forgotten in such work that problems of vision and/or visibility may easily arise.

(5) A first reading may sometimes be done by asking the class to read in unison. Some students will of course be 'passengers' every now and then, but this does not matter if the follow-up reading is made

individual and the teacher, who will have noted the 'passengers', asks them for the repetition, each taking about 10 outlines to some convenient changeover point in the piece.

(6) Preparation for reading is a most useful out-of-class activity. The time when the reading will be required should be specified, and when it arrives the teacher should have a key (preferably marked in tens) so that stop-watch calculation of the speed attained is easy and the student can be informed at once of the level of her success. Regular, but not too frequent (once a week), use of this technique will often produce excellent results with a considerable competitive element spontaneously arising. Do not make any attempt to force it and pass no strictures on the less successful; instead, find something encouraging to say about the clarity or the audibility or any other aspect of the performance that arises. Students should get to know at a fairly early stage what their reading ability is, and be encouraged to improve it.

(7) Requiring students to read from their own notes when these have been recorded from dictation and not copied is, of course, a most necessary activity. What it is most necessary to concentrate on here is self-criticism. If the student is only partly successful then she should be asked to ring any outline where she had temporary difficulty or complete failure and then to find out *why* it was that she could not read her own note. In the answers to these questions will lie the improvement of the student's own shorthand.

(8) A further useful technique is to ask the students to read silently to a certain point and then to indicate when they reach this point by raising a hand. Those who reach this point are told to re-read from the beginning again, while waiting for the rest of the students. The technique can be varied by giving a specified time like two minutes, and then at the end of that time to find out who has got farthest.

When the reading is called for, those who did not complete the piece, or who did not get very far, should be called upon first. In using this technique, the author allows each student one question. The student does not say it but calls the teacher's attention by standing up. The teacher then goes to the student and gives her the spoken word required for the outline.

Copying shorthand: the workbook principle

There are several reasons for copying shorthand—as an aid to speed building, as an aid to improve the accuracy and style of the shorthand writing, and as a way of increasing familiarity with, and automaticity in, vocabulary.

As for the ways in which the copying may take place, the most important is that based on the workbook principle.

(1) Either the shorthand to be copied may be written carefully but cursively and at no required speed into a shorthand notebook, each line being followed by two blank lines, or the workbook may be printed ready for use, the shorthand being shown in 'copperplate' or in excellent facsimile. The principle is that every textbook exercise should, after it has been read, be written into shorthand at set speeds from audio, this method not only ensuring that the students work continuously from correct shorthand but that the teacher is freed to observe, help and guide the individual students. Learning and practice conducted in this way has been proved to be very effective and economical of time. When a workbook is provided, then its use should be an indispensable part of the learning process.

(2) In the later stages of theory learning and in speed development, copying by writing over an existing line of shorthand again and again in order to develop increasing speed is a useful technique. It is important in this, as in all other copying, that there should be an aural or a mental intellectual link between the visual—what is being copied—and the meaning of the symbols.

(3) Fair copying from printed shorthand (as from *2000*) is useful in the theory-learning stages to build up the mental images of correct shorthand and later on as preparation for dictation. Once again, care must be taken to ensure that the students are mentally reading and not mindlessly copying.

Short forms
The arbitraries of the system have to be so learned and so absorbed that they become almost as much an automaticized response to a stimulus as signing one's name to a letter. In New Era there are well over 300 of them; in Pitman 2000 fewer than 100. All must be over-learned—the psychologists' term for that condition of learning when you have gone beyond mere recall or response and continue to go on learning and practising until conscious recall is unnecessary and response seemingly no longer needs any deliberate act of the mind to evoke it.

Complete command of the short forms is vital for speed and accuracy of transcript. It follows that the short forms have to be practised and drilled in every teaching unit. New ones will need to be learned as the theory knowledge advances and those already learned will have to be continually exercised.

The principle that it is best to learn in the form in which final use occurs suggests that the best way to exercise short forms is in sentences and paragraphs. We compose easy sentences to include and repeat a number of times those particular short forms which are the object of our immediate learning. Then we read the sentences and dictate them, re-read and re-dictate alternately at increasing speeds. This is one aspect of the 'drill' element.

In the original learning, when the student comes upon the short forms for the first time, it will be natural to make a list. It is important that the order of the words in such a list is continually changed; otherwise unwanted associations will be built up which may easily inhibit the desired kind of learning. The classic instance, known to most teachers of New Era, is the 'with-when-what-would' syndrome. In Pitman 2000, this does not occur.

Suppose the group of short forms to be learned happens to be: *particular, with, your, his, it, knowledge, any, large*. Then an excellent initial method of learning is to array these down the page in a one-inch column. Leave a blank column and array them again, only this time work alternately from the bottom of the list then the top, viz. *large, particular, any, with, knowledge, your* etc. Leave another blank column and once again work alternately from bottom then top. In this way no two short forms will come to have unwanted associations. Twelve such columns (six practices) can be so arranged on an A4 sheet turned longways—'landscape'—wise.

A second form of drill, more intensive in its nature, that should follow the two already described is to dictate groups of short forms, ten or twenty at a time, four or five times at a fixed rate of speed—the same short forms but in a different order at each repetition. This method is 'unnatural' but it serves to sharply focus the students' attention on the short forms that are to be learned and equally sharply to give them experience of what 'knowing' the short forms really means: automatic and correct response to single-word stimulus at 80 wam. This drill method is part of the workbook principle discussed earlier.

There is a further point to be observed in the continual revision and consolidation of the short forms: none ought to be left unrevised and unpractised for very long. We have, therefore, to build up a cyclic scheme for drill and practice which constantly brings back 'old' short forms, especially those which we know students have trouble in mastering.

Phrasing
The advantages of phrasing are obvious to us as teachers, but less so to the students who need to be clearly shown the benefits.

It is true that there are many phrases arising from the very high frequency collocations of words (*of the, and the, and as, it is,* etc.)

that might be considered as standard outlines and so taught.

But from the student's viewpoint, a proper understanding of the principles of phrasing is the important thing to know. All teachers should study the *locus classicus* for phrasing, *The New Phonographic Phrasebook*, Emily D. Smith (Pitman),* to establish more widely their own understanding of the subject. Even at the earliest stage students should be encouraged to use the natural phrases, and copied dictation and prepared dictation should take cognisance of the phrasing opportunities, and the passages spoken, to deliberately steer them into phrase writing. It is also an added reason for dictating in quick, natural groups of words with intervals of silence in between which enable the student to perceive the outline for the phrase before the pen has already begun to shape a series of words instead.

Without demanding that students learn phrases by heart like short forms, the same kind of contextual practice is desirable when some new phrasing principle has been presented. For example, if the students have just learned that 'us' in a phrase may be a circle **S**, then they can first read, then copy, then dictate, sentences like these:

Tell us what you can do for us and let us meet soon.
It is not for us to say who will be with us; we hope you will help us.

Writing shorthand

The principles of penmanship have already been discussed. Some methods for concentrating attention on it and for successful learning are now suggested.

(1) A speed exercise which students like and which aims directly at maintaining good penmanship after practice is the following. Compose a sentence of exactly twenty words including two good phrases and one or two of the words that we know from experience students find it hard to write well (summer, children, discovery, indicate, quiet), e.g. *In summer we hope to be able to see the children if we can get time off for the trip.* These twelve outlines can be written on a single line of the notebook in correct shorthand. Paced copy drills in 20 seconds (60), 15 seconds (80), 12 seconds (100), 10 seconds (120) can then be carried out. These are followed by a 30-second drill, the object throughout being to write each line of the shorthand with a uniformity and accuracy equal to that of the original.

(2) Single word and phrase drills are good for boosting confidence. Four or five of these timed for only 15 or 20 seconds each will occupy only a minute or two, but they will get much repetitive work and

* Also appearing as *Guide to Phrasing*.

over-learning done with a purpose. The drills should only occasionally be regarded as competitive, but rather as devoted to the improvement of previous individual achievement.

(3) Occasionally, time should be devoted to writing only for style. Convert an interesting piece of about 100 words into shorthand and have it copied carefully by the students, preferably from an electronic stencil. Use it for two minutes each day as a reading and copying exercise until it is thoroughly known. On the fourth or fifth day dictate it at a speed comfortable for all and have the work done on a looseleaf sheet. Then collect these and assess them for the writing only, dealing with any points noted on a 2-in. margin left on the sheets.

Word frequency
During the early learning of shorthand a restriction to a limited vocabulary is a wise principle. The student has much to learn in a short time: new symbols, their meanings, how to combine them and write them at an acceptable speed. To this problem we do not wish to add that of an unrestricted vocabulary at the same time. The fewer the number of words we can base all our theory and penmanship requirements on, the quicker and more lasting will be the learning. Basic texts, therefore, are generally confined to 1,000–2,000 words. A great deal of material both in longhand and shorthand has been provided for students, within the 700 Common Words series, and this is constantly useful during, and for a brief time after, the initial learning stage.

Thereafter its value as the base for speed development declines rapidly. By this time students are familiar with the common words; this is inevitable because the words *are* common. Moreover, the kind of subjects that can be dealt with within the framework of the common words, and the inevitably dull and lifeless English that may be their concomitant, make little appeal to the student. Continuing use of common-word material will give them an optimistically false idea of their ability.

On the other hand, the plunge from a severely controlled vocabulary to an unrestricted one is likely to exercise a frustrating and dis-motivating effect on the student who is eager to get on to 70, 80 and 90 wam. Probably the best plan is to use common-word material up to the 60–70 stage but add appropriate increments of frequently occurring, but not so common words, at each level of theory knowledge. *Dictation Practice* uses this principle in the (*b*) and (*c*) passages in the learning of Pitman 2000.

Vowels
The vowels have always been to some degree a controversial area in the

study and teaching of Pitman shorthand. The questions debated are: How should the vowels be taught? When should they be discarded and to what extent? How can we best link the vowels with position?

Generally, teachers introduce the vowels one or two at a time, at the same time as the consonants are introduced, four or five or more at a time. In the early stages of learning some practice is essential to ensure that the students can distinguish the vowels readily one from another, and that each is firmly connected with its position. Students will also have to learn for the most part to ignore spelling and go only by the sounds of the words. One way is to cover a 1 ... 2 ... 3 group of vowels like *ah, ay, ee* (*car, lay, tea*) and connect them with their positions both in the placing of the vowel and in the placing of the first upstroke, downstroke or horizontal. For this purpose, single and two-stroke outlines can be used, like *calm, take, teach*, and *ma, day, fee*. Presenting all the positions in one group has its advantages, both in grasping the idea of position and in making a considerable range of common words available.

The students also have to acquire a new writing habit—that of executing the consonantal skeleton of a word at one lift of the pen and then, contrary to handwriting practice, inserting the vowels immediately after completing the words. Students often find this strange at first. A different approach is to dispense with the old mnemonics, 'Pa may we all go too', 'That pen is not much good', 'I now enjoy music' and to use a different set like 'Mark all that lot by boys', 'Pay Joe ten bucks' and 'Please do this book, Hugh, now', thus bringing all the vowel and diphthong signs of one position together and teaching one position at a time, usually in the order 2 ... 1 ... 3. Diphones (double vowels) and triphones (treble vowels) may be brought in at the same time or immediately after. Both of these basic methods have their adherents and the advantage here is the strong positional sense that is acquired by the students.

If, as the author believes, it is a realistic practice to drop lightly stressed and neuter vowels straight away once copying and dictation are begun, then a brief practice in each lesson should be given in vocalization, outlines being given and the students asked to copy and then fully vocalize them. Some teachers are ardent advocates of not teaching the vowels at all—as vowels—in the initial stages, but connecting sound directly with position.

The true answer to the question of when they should be discarded is 'Never'. Even at high speeds expert shorthand writers will find time for the occasional vowel, especially initial or final vowels not otherwise indicated by the outline, and diphthongs and diphones. But on the other hand, the great majority of consonantal outlines are either so distinctive or can be so easily read by context that for most of the time vowels can be omitted and, as soon as some familiarity with outlines has been established, they should be. There is no need for continual insertion of vowels in writing shorthand, but they should remain for a longer period as 'recognition signs' and as an aid to quick reading in exercise material.

The speed-development stage

When well-taught students reach the end of their initial learning of the system, they will be writing on familiar material at 50 or 60 wam. From this point we may say that the course has changed gear. There will be little apparent difference at first, but gradually the balance of the teaching-unit content will change. There will be less systematic and more incidental study of the theory, a greater preparation of dictation and a slowly rising proportion of this will be 'free'—that is, not previously read, prepared or dictated. On the other hand, there will still be much reading of advanced-style, unrestricted vocabulary shorthand—both copperplate and facsimile; much of the dictation will be prepared; there will continue to be penmanship and short-form drills; the theory will continue to be studied but in a different way; facility drills and workbook-copied dictation will still be of some importance.

Theory during speed development

'Speed from the beginning and theory all the time' is an old adage of the shorthand world, and it embodies a true teaching principle of a time-skill. Today, the way to continue and expand theoretical knowledge is to use a follow-up book (such as *New Review of Pitman's Shorthand* in New Era or the Pitman 2000 equivalent) which presents the same knowledge as a first course but in a quite different way, assuming a total knowledge and therefore not confining examples to those that do not anticipate other principles not yet dealt with. In addition, it seeks new approaches to the theory and expands knowledge and amplifies understanding. During the 50—80+ stage, therefore, a new look at principles is taken and some time devoted to reading, writing and copying from this text in each teaching unit.

A different but equally useful way of understanding the reasons for writing an outline in this, rather than that way, and for re-emphasizing principles, is the incidental treatment of particular ones as they occur in material to be read or taken from dictation. In a group of words like this,

for example: _____ , we might ask what are the

principles involved in writing the word *fossils* and get replies such as: 'The first downstroke is above the line because the first vowel is ŏ—a short first-position vowel' and 'When a circle occurs between two curved strokes it is written inside the first curve'; at which point we might dictate a few words like *vessel, nasal, Kingsley*.

Dictation

At the core of all shorthand learning is dictation. During the speed-development stage it becomes of dominant importance but the matters now to be discussed are for the most part applicable from the beginning of study. There are three possible sources of input for the shorthand writer, the spoken word, the visual stimulus of print or handwriting and one's own thoughts given a permanent form in written symbols. Because of the usual applications of the shorthand skill the first of these is by far the most important and this is the one to which we shall now give our attention.

For the teacher there are two main ways of giving dictation: the first is the teacher's own dictation to the students and the second is the indirect method of audio which may be either commercially produced or 'home-made' by the teacher. Both of these methods should be used, the first because it will enable the teacher to employ a variety of different techniques according to need, and the second because it will free the teacher from the task (which can be quite onerous) of dictating in order to observe, guide and help the individual learners.

Other possible ways are to use students themselves for dictation, or to use appropriate radio or TV pieces, or to bring in other teachers to accustom students to different voices and accents.

Manner of dictating

How dictation is given is very important. High-speed writers will tell you that the difference in ability of the dictator can easily make a difference of at least ten words a minute in attainment; at lower levels, it is equally important. What we have to remember is that we are teaching our students to respond to the aural stimulus and therefore the dictation should be the best that can possibly be given. When learning shorthand, students have a right to require the best conditions possible and excellence of dictation is one such condition.

What are the characteristics of good dictation?

(1) The words should be clearly articulated, especially the little linking words that are often slurred over in everyday speech. This does not mean, however, an exaggerated or over-meticulous articulation that

will be retro-active by calling attention to itself instead of to the meaning and the content.

(2) The words should be spoken naturally, not in a special 'dictation voice'. The only satisfactory and salutary way to check this is to listen to your own voice by recording a piece for dictation and writing shorthand from it.

(3) Words should be spoken quickly but clearly in natural groups with intervals of silence; it is a fault of technique to try to fill all the available time with sound, and this applies equally at 50 wam as at 120 wam. The natural groups of words should be those that correspond with the meaning and with the sentence structure. For example, in such a sentence as: When the prices/of all items of food// are rising/ at such a rapid rate,// it is not surprising/ that there should be// repeated demands by workers/ for higher wages.//, these groups are indicated by the soliduses, the single ones those that might be used at 50–70 wam and the double ones those that should be used not only for these lower speeds but for 100 wam or above. Students at the lower speeds have not yet acquired enough experience to store long groups, but later on groups of eight or more words are quite comfortably retained. There are several advantages to this manner of dictation: the first is that it is less likely to be boring; the second is that it enables the writer to write 'behind' the dictation and thus phrase well; the third is that the meaning is better conveyed in this way.

(4) The dictation should be given with a pleasant variety of pitch and emphasis, but 'expression' or an emotive element ought not to be introduced because this is distracting and may militate against the writer instead of for her.

(5) The words should be spoken at a consistent speed and (generally) precision-timed by a stopwatch. An even speed is a significant aid to the writer.

(6) Every opportunity should be taken during the learning process to help the shorthand writer by a vocal indication of convenient phrasing. For example, confronted by this sentence:

These birds are found *in all parts of the world*//but were observed *for the first time*//in Spain *two or three* years ago.

an experienced dictator would make gaps of silence at the double soliduses, but would also make momentary pauses at the spaces, and run together, at a little faster rate, the italicized words. It is important, of course, that this should not be overdone so that the dictation appears unnatural; after about 80 wam it will be unnecessary and impracticable, anyway.

(7) Some dictation ought to be given untimed—even extempore occasionally. In the realistic situation, students will never be called upon to work from timed dictation and indeed the words will often be cancelled or amended and new material interpolated: this is what is commonly termed 'office style' dictation. It should, in the opinion of the author, be reserved for a very late stage in the course and, particularly, during transcription training.

(8) A further way in which the dictation may be given to assist the learner is by studying the passage beforehand, noting the position where writing difficulty may occur, and arranging to slow at that point, speeding up slightly in an easier part.

(9) All shorthand dictation for training should be flawless. Mistakes, 'fluffs' (momentary false starts) and corrections hinder the writer at any speed and in high-speed tests can destroy the chances of success of the writer.

Test dictation

Passages to test students' ability under examination conditions should be characterized by:

(1) The syllabic level of 1·4–1·5 in each half-minute of the test passage, this being the standard English level (i.e. 142 syllables to 100 words).

(2) A vocabulary, if not within a circumscribed word frequency, at least within what might be accepted as 'average English', without any uncommon technical words (*gasket, hygrometer, metallurgy*), archaic words (*winnowing, flail*) or unusual words (*carphology, esoteric, parameter*), and with no proper nouns or adjectives outside those that may be regarded as within the recognition and recall range of any average person (e.g. *Great Britain, French* would be reasonable, but *Alcibiades* and *sapphic* would not).

(3) Sentence structures that do not introduce too many difficulties for the writers. Those of the following types often present difficulty: series of words or phrases of the same functional type; inversions; long sentences with involved compound-complex structure; periodic sentences; parenthetic structures.

Techniques of dictation

In addition to untimed and irregular dictation of the kind to be used for part of the available time, and the normal strictly-timed plain dictation at a given speed in words a minute, there are other variations of the dictation technique, all of which have their uses at different times according to the student need.

(*a*) *Copied dictation* This technique is still a most useful one in preparing passages for subsequent free dictation. At the speed stage it is much easier for the students, who will now have a reasonable familiarity with shorthand and feel comfortable writing it, to copy direct from book or periodical. The notebook should be close up to the passage being copied and on the right of it (for right-handed writers). The two or three blank-line method is also still very relevant.

(*b*) *Changing-speed dictation* The dictation at the beginning is at a speed which most students find fairly easy but after half a minute it is increased by 20 wam and then after another half-minute reverts to the original. This technique is useful for training students to sustain intensive bursts and to get used to working at speeds that briefly put them under pressure.

(*c*) *Repetition dictation* The idea of the repetition is, of course, that the increasing familiarity will help to make the speed pressure less and enable the student to write better outlines. Various slightly different techniques can be adapted from the plain one of dividing, say, a three-minute piece into six approximately half-minute lengths, **ABCDEF** and then dictating **A** and **B**—pause—dictate **B** and **C**—pause—dictate **C** and **D** and so on. Another way is to dictate **A** first at the average class speed then repeated at ten or even twenty words faster. On this repetition go straight on to **B**, only this half-minute slows down to the original speed. Next dictate **B** and **C**, **B** at the 10/20 words faster rate and **C** at the lower rate—and so on.

(*d*) *Breakdown* As an occasional reinforcement of determination and stamina this is a challenging exercise. You dictate for not longer than two minutes at a time, beginning at a speed which the whole group can manage—say 80 wam—and then raise the second half-minute to 100, the third to 120, the fourth to 140. The students are told to hold on but to stop when they can no longer take *every* word. After two minutes you check where each student has given up, have the most successful read back last, of course, and then repeat the passage at a steady speed before giving the breakdown just once more. It should not be continued beyond a single repeat.

(*e*) *Storage* Students vary naturally in their ability to retain words verbatim for reproduction in shorthand. It is a necessary talent, and fortunately it can be trained.
Even in the early learning stages it is worth occasional practice; in

speed development it becomes increasingly important. A short 2–3 minute drill used once or twice a week is quite effective. The teacher composes sentences of precise length like this:

No-one was in when I called yesterday (8).
If I can make the time I will call again (10).
This will not be until Monday of next week at the earliest (12).
There is no reason why the call should not produce an order (12).
Last time he asked us to supply goods up to £1,500 value (14).
I am sorry I did not call before but I did not know the shop was in my sales area (20).

The sentences are dictated but the students do not begin until the word 'Write!' at the end. A useful variation of this is to write a short paragraph of fifty or sixty words for dictation at the class speed, the students not being allowed to write until the first ten or twelve have been uttered.

(f) *'Seen passage'* It is surprising that this excellent technique, devised and proved highly effective by Squire Flitcroft in Chesterfield, should not be more widely known and used. The principle is that of total familiarity and over-learning, producing a high positive transfer in speed and accuracy of shorthand.

The first thing is to choose—or better still adapt and write—a suitable passage of about 1,000–1,200 words. The criteria should be: a general non-specialized business and/or topical vocabulary, average difficulty (free of those speed difficulties to which attention has already been called) and providing plenty of good shorthand phrasing opportunities.

Then you prepare this in excellent facsimile shorthand which can be cheaply reproduced by electronic stencil. Alternatively, an appropriate passage from *Memo* or *2000* may be used.

Each student must have and retain the facsimile shorthand for reference and out-of-class preparation. Let us suppose that at the time you begin practice, the class is already writing at 70–90 wam. Then you proceed as follows:

(i) Read the whole piece to the students but not all at once. Two minutes' reading is long enough initially.

(ii) Students re-read aloud after you, using any reading technique you wish to adopt.

(iii) Students copy the shorthand of the first 200 words to your slow dictation at about 60 wam.

(iv) The piece is repeated at 80 wam and the shorthand re-checked.

(v) The piece is re-dictated at 80, and 50 more words from the passage are added at a lower speed.

(vi) This process continues, the first 100 words of the passage being dictated at 90, 100, 110, 120 etc. wam and the next 100–150 words at declining speeds, until the day's increment of 50 words goes back to 80 wam.

(vii) As the build-up grows larger, it will be necessary to divide the piece first into two passages and later into three, rotating these on each of three successive days and continuing to build up the speed.

By this method it is possible to get students writing successfully at speeds of 40 and 50 wam above their 'true' speed. The motivation produced by this achievement always outweighs the boredom that it might be supposed would arise from such long-continued repetition. The use of the passage from the time when it is first begun to the time when it is eventually abandoned can easily be as long as 30–50 working days; it requires about 10 minutes of attention each day plus some out-of-class time. The effect on the actual 'free' dictation of the students is considerable: they are much more confident having the knowledge that they *can* write at these much higher speeds, their digital and manual ability is improved, and from 'free' dictation they write better and faster in consequence.

Content of dictation

At the speed-development stage, what to dictate is an important consideration. Since the proportion of time spent on dictation in one form or another is increasing, and the students' speed is rising too, the total volume of material required is considerable.

The interests of the students require that a good deal of the material should be of a business and a general topical kind. The great majority will be working in offices of some kind, and although we cannot provide for their specialist needs we have to ensure that they get ample practice on the vocabulary and phrasing applicable to all business communications.

We must also have regard to the kind of material provided for examinations and here we need to assemble a good stock of recent past papers not usually going back for more than five years, and kept constantly up-to-date.

The textbook in use as a follow-up to the first course will also provide much material for dictation and so will the weekly shorthand pages of *2000*, keyed in *Office Skills*.

But a diet restricted to these sources of supply would tend to be an arid one. It is equally in the interests of our students, both from the viewpoint of their general education and of keeping up their interest and motivation, that we draw material from a wider field and it is in this area that the teacher can be of greatest service to her students. The available material is almost limitless and the selection from it is a difficult but essential task.

The following are suggestions only, but offer guidelines for selection. Passages chosen ought not usually to exceed 200–300 words if sufficient variety is to be introduced.

Literature: passages chosen because of their beauty or because of the philosophical ideas and concepts of value that they embody.

Poetry: the poetry of such moderns as Cecil Day Lewis, W. H. Auden, Ogden Nash often provide items that will appeal even to average students.

Anecdotes: brief, well-written stories with a punch line.

Fiction: suitable passages drawn from the works of modern writers like Nabokov, Saul Bellow, Kingsley Amis, Mary Renault, John Fowles.

Articles: extracts from good popular journalism such as *The Listener*, the weekly colour supplements, the magazines and periodicals, the whole world of the *feuilleton*.

Documentaries: extracts from the publications of HMSO, from books that deal with topical subjects of value like *The Sea Around Us* (Ruth Carson), the weather, the aviation industry, commodities, transport, social welfare, leisure activities, fashion, holidays, travel, advertising, consumer information—the list is endless.

Preparing for dictation

During the stage 60–100 wam at least, it is still necessary to ensure that a large part of the dictation given should be prepared beforehand. Students required to build their speed on imperfect knowledge and skill will quickly form wrong habits, writing incorrect outlines in a degenerating style. Preparation is the insurance against this happening; to what extent and by what methods to prepare must depend on the teacher's judgement of the class needs. The suggestions that follow must be viewed in that light.

Suppose the passage to be prepared is of 300 words and either it is available in 'copperplate' or facsimile in *2000*, or it has already been written and run off by an electronic stencil. Ten minutes' preliminary study will enable the teacher to devise a preparation plan for dealing with the passage. That plan might be as follows:

(*a*) Preparation beforehand by the teacher. Read through the shorthand; then read again, this time selecting words that may not be familiar enough to be written automatically by the students, short forms to be drilled, phrases that may need practice, any interpretation of meaning that may be necessary for the students' full understanding. List all these items.

(*b*) The students all have a copy of the correct shorthand. Read it to them sentence by sentence, requiring a named student to repeat each sentence. At the end of this, have the passage read again, partly in unison, partly by individuals.

(*c*) On the completion of the second reading write up and get the students to copy and read back the outlines you have selected. Drill the short forms two or three times, asking students to arrange them in different orders and dictate them to the class. Deal with any words, idioms or technical terms that you judge to need attention. By question and answer discuss any points of theory that are judged to be necessary.

(*d*) Divide the piece roughly into three sections. Have the students copy the first section of the passage from their original, leaving each alternate line blank; this may either be untimed, the students writing for accuracy and style, or it may be copied at a set slow speed. Now the students copy again, on the blank line, but this time the speed will be given by three or four students who dictate aloud while themselves copying. The rest of the class must be observed while at work, their aim being to keep up with the dictating student and not falling behind or going ahead. They must understand that what they are doing is practising the writing while associating the spoken words with the outlines as they write them.

(*e*) At this point the students turn to a fresh page of their notebook and record the first section from a dictated note at a speed which will enable all or almost all of them to record a full note. This actual note must now be read back and the students required to check it carefully against the original shorthand.

(*f*) Now (*d*) and (*e*) may be repeated for the second and the third section. Alternatively, step (*g*) may now be taken.

(*g*) Each section is now re-dictated at 10 or 20 wam above the speed of the initial dictation and the degree of success of the students in achieving a full note checked.

(*h*) The final stage is the dictation of the entire passage at a speed first 10 and then 20 wam above the speed of the original. These notes should be read back as far as is necessary to check how well the students have succeeded in attaining their known goal.

It is obvious that this method of preparation is thorough, comprehensive and exhaustive. With good students or an easier passage it may be possible to telescope or omit some of these stages. Sometimes they should be asked to read their neighbour's note instead of their own; they should also practise their own weak outlines. If the preparation is for ultimate typed transcription then it will need further modification, but these points will be dealt with in Chapter 8 on Transcription.

Speed and speed forcing

The natural desire of the teacher and of the students will be to raise the speed of dictation. However, a careful balance will have to be kept to ensure that the students are not too often being obliged to write at a pace where their outlines break down or they are forced to make omissions. Only the teacher can preserve this balance by careful observation of what the students are doing. Since the only way of progress is by attempting now what you could not do before, there must be times when students are at the limit of their capacity; it is at this time that they need to be encouraged to persist, never to give up even if they have to leave a gap sometimes. the importance of preparation as a means of building and then consolidating speed will then become clear. Periods of maximum effort must alternate with periods of less intensive effort—but effort all the same.

Short bursts of one minute above the 'true' speed of the students can often be successful, and then step by step the progress made can be consolidated before another reach forward in speed is attempted.

Plateaux

When time-skill training is efficiently and intensively conducted, there is not very much evidence of plateaux of learning forming. By a plateau is meant a stage of development in the skill where the learner finds it difficult to progress further. The following extract from Harm Harms' book *Methods in Vocational Business Education* (South Western Publishing Company, 1949) is relevant:

> The reasons for plateaux are many: fatigue, emotional disturbances, wrong technique in connection with some particular phase of the work, etc. The basic observation in connection with plateaux is that it represents a stage in learning when the organism is endeavouring to change from one level of reacting to a higher and better organized

level. Psychologists maintain that if the skill is presented in such a way that the higher level characteristics are embodied in the beginning techniques, then the organism will not have to unlearn one set of patterns to form another . . .

Woodworth gives the causes of plateaux as:

. . . (1) undue attention to one part of the task, (2) oscillation of attention from one part to another, (3) conscious effort to co-ordinate, (4) carrying over of errors from one part of the performance to another (as in a two-handed performance), and (5) lack of balance between the skill attained in different parts of a complex skill.

Commins urges: 'Many plateaux may be broken by an increase in the strength of motivation. The fact that improvement may not be as great as originally expected may give rise to discouragement and a subsequent "going stale".'

Smith, in a study of the causes of plateaux in learning, came to the conclusion that about 60 per cent of them are due to such factors as failure in motivation, emotional strain, weather, light, illness and relearning after a period of inactivity, and Gates has said: 'It is particularly important in the early stages of learning to detect errors, which, if allowed to persist, may become difficult to break and may impede progress or make it impossible. By controlling motivation, the organization of units of instruction and learning procedures, teachers and students together may prevent many plateaux.' *

Individual differences: lack of homogeneity

It is at this stage in development when differences in the level of attainment become most vexatious. As the students become steadily more familiar with the system and with writing it at speed, the gap between the best and the worst will tend to widen. When this situation arises, the teacher is faced with a problem not easy to solve. Even when every effort is made by persuading students at the lower end of the scale to do more work outside the class, and to give them special help and guidance and to hold the class together if possible, it may still happen that the naturally quick will outrun their fellow students to the point where group working will need to be resorted to. If a flexible promotion and relegation scheme is possible, this will solve the difficulty.

---

* Harm Harms, *Methods in Vocational Business Education* (South Western Publishing Company, 1949). Details of the references appear in the book.

It may well be that we have a new weapon through the resources of educational technology to cope better with the problem while still maintaining the class organization. A range of cassettes (C60), giving about 56 minutes of dictation on two tracks, could be prepared covering exactly the same material, about two-thirds of which could be of business content and one-third on more general topics. This range could be at speeds of 70 wam (which is where the problem of lack of homogeneity begins to make itself felt) in steps of 10 wam all the way up to 120 wam. These cassettes could be played on the cheap but very efficient, easy-to-operate playback-only machines now commercially available, free-standing, portable and battery-operated. It would now be possible to work as a class so far as preparation, copying and reading back was concerned but to provide exactly the right speed slot for each individual. Such a development would be of the greatest help to all teachers facing the problem of differing levels of shorthand speed attainment.

7 Teaching Audio-Typing

The teaching of audio-typing has not yet become as systematized as the teaching of typewriting or shorthand. Indeed, it is not taught at all in some schools and colleges, or only in a perfunctory and partial way. For example, four or five students from a typewriting class may be selected for a week's course on the available machines, and then replaced at the end of that time by a further group.

One reason for this lack of attention must be the shortage of money to provide machines and the lack (until now) of the necessary software in the form of cassettes, tapes, cylinders etc. Another reason may well be doubts in the minds of teachers and educationists of the extent to which the claims about the virtues of audio-typing by manufacturers of the machines are true.

It is often believed that all that a competent typist needs to do in order to become an equally competent audio-typist is to learn how to operate the transcriber efficiently and listen to the audio recording and then type from it. This is far from the truth.

The nature of the skills of typing and audio-typing is different. The audio-typist needs, as one component of her total skill, a competence in typing. But over and above that she needs a range of knowledge and sub-skills that are not demanded from the typist, plus the totally new skill of listen-and-type.

Before the questions of aims, equipment, standards of attainment and teaching methods are discussed, it will be relevant to consider what are the particular problems that face the audio-typist.

Audio-typing problems

(1) An audio-typist has to work from an ephemeral input; the typist has her copy to work from and it stays there as a permanent visual stimulus; the shorthand-typist produces a symbolic written record which then becomes the permanent visual stimulus. The audio-typist hears the words and then they are gone. It is true she has a machine which will

enable her to replay words and phrases, but it is likely that if she did not understand the aural input the first time then she will not understand the second; such repetition will only sometimes bring enlightenment and if such replays often become necessary, then the supposed advantages of audio-typing are at once dissipated.

(2) The spoken word through the medium of an electronic machine is less effective than the spoken word in the direct face-to-face situation. There are two reasons for this: the first is that however good the reproduction qualities of the machine in use are, they can never be so good as the original utterance; the second is that hearing speech at a remove from the speaker always tends towards a less effective communication. You may talk to your loved one on the telephone but that is never as good as talking to her face to face: you miss the gesture, the facial expression, the attitude, even some of the subtlety of intonation, all of which in a person-to-person conversation count for much in increasing the effectiveness of the communication.

(3) The audio-typist has no prior knowledge before she begins transcribing what the communication is all about; a shorthand-typist or a typist has. The audio-typist initially does not know whether she has to cope with a letter, a memorandum or a report, what the subject of it is, what length it is, how many copies will be needed, what special instructions relate to it, what the relevant back-up or explanatory documents are. All this information has to be given to her by some means or another before she can begin, and there must be no error or omission, otherwise it will all have to be done again.

(4) At any point within the communication, the audio-typist does not know what is coming next, nor does she know very often what conventions of visual representation are required of her in dealing with particular items. Suppose, for example, she hears: 'We have asked for 400 bales of cotton waste at present held in the Straits Warehouse to be loaded on to mv *Stella Polaris* lying in Dock 4 on Monday next 17 March. Bound first for Alexandria, the vessel is due to sail on Wednesday 19 March.' Now how is she to cope with the number of bales (figures or words)? Will she be sure to know that it is 'waste' not 'waist' and 'sail' not 'sale'? Until she has heard it through she might easily type 'Straits' with a lower-case letter, as well as being in doubt which Straits (straights? Strate's?) were being referred to. What is she to do about 'Dock 4'—lower case? letters for 4? It is not until she gets to 'is due' that she will realize that there should have been a full stop at 'March.' What shall she do about 'mv', and is she to be expected to know the Latin for North Star is 'Stella Polaris'?

For such reasons as these it has become necessary to make use of

standard dictating conventions (referred to below) and to incorporate all
these instructions into the actual dictation to ensure (or try to ensure)
that the audio-typist does not make an understandable error only to find
out too late what she ought to have typed.

(5) It is only rarely that the audio-typist has any direct involvement
in the origination of the message. The shorthand-typist, on the other
hand, has this involvement: she is making her personal contribution to
it and can often by a question or a comment assist in its composition,
sometimes to a significant extent. The involvement itself is motivating
and gives the shorthand-typist a valuable sense of satisfaction and of
achievement in her work; her feelings of self-confidence and of personal
prestige are enhanced by it.

(6) If the audio-typist is engaged exclusively in the audio-typing activity—and this is frequently so in business—she is for a large part of
her day shut off from communication with the outside because the
headset shuts her into a little claustrophobic world; she has a much
more restricted field of human contact in her business life than her
fellow-workers in the office skills. This is a factor of real significance: it
is sufficient by itself to account for the fact shown in a recent survey by
the Alfred Marks Bureau, who publish quarterly through their
Statistical Services Division a most valuable and interesting investigation into all aspects of the business life of office-skills workers, that 70
per cent of audio-typists were dissatisfied with their jobs and wished to
move out of them. Girls like to be working with men and vice versa; we
are gregarious and like to find ourselves in like-minded and interest-
sharing groups.

(7) When faced with difficulties of comprehension or interpretation
the shorthand-typist is able to ask immediate questions or look up
references before beginning the work of transcription; her permanent
visual record enables her to do this. The audio-typist has no such opportunities. The author believes that one consequence of this fact is that the
audio-typist ought to (but usually will not) be able to call upon a larger
vocabulary and a wider general knowledge than the shorthand-typist.

(8) In order to do her work, the audio-typist is dependent upon a
power supply and the mechanical and electrical devices of a machine,
the operational requirements, maintenance, breakdowns or errors of
which to some extent restrict and increase the difficulty of her work.
Imperfections in recording and above all the quality of the dictation that
is provided by the originators from which she has to work have an even
greater effect upon her output than similar considerations do on the
work of the shorthand-typist. For the latter, it is easier to make up for
deficiencies in the dictation by queries on the spot, and as the tools of

her trade consist of nothing but a notebook and a good pen, difficulties are minimal.

One point of significance that emerges from this survey is that the supposed economy of audio-typing when compared with shorthand-typing is illusory. What in fact happens is that many of the responsibilities that the shorthand-typist can take in her stride devolve upon the originator, who is called upon to structure his recording so that it shall be free of ambiguity at every point, not only so far as the actual communication is concerned but in all the attendant details as well. The work of the originator is increased both in time and difficulty when he is working via audio instead of via shorthand (see also the section below on the nature of the dictation for audio-typing) and this is a factor not sufficiently taken into account either in the office or in the training situation.

There is a real need for specific training for originators of audio input. Difficulties and problems are not insoluble and enlightened employers find means of solving them both on the originators' and the operatives' side. One successful solution is not to require an audio-typist to work wholly and exclusively at audio-typing but to include in her work other activities that take her away from the machine, give her a more positive interest in work and enable her to have more human contacts. On the training side it would be both more helpful and relevant to national needs if office-skills workers were not regarded as falling into one category or another; the need is for those who are equally skilled in all aspects of communication and record. The shorthand/audio dichotomy ought to be abandoned; office-skills workers should be well trained in shorthand, typewriting, audio-typing, transcription, filing, calculations, the use of the telephone and above all have a high standard of linguistic ability. These last are dealt with in detail in Chapter 8.

The skill of audio-typing: aims

The first aim of an audio-typing course will be to give students specific training in the new skill of listen-and-type. The natural reaction of a reasonably competent typist when first faced with audio-typing is to listen to a few words, stop the machine and then to record these words, before going back to the machine to listen to more words, pause, then record them, and so on in a series of kangaroo hops. Students must not be allowed to get into this habit; they have to be trained to listen-and-type continuously. Since the speed of the dictation may be at 80 wam or above and the speed of the typist when employed on direct transcribing (as opposed to plain copy-typing) only 30–40 wam, this means that the student has to learn to store words mentally and to acquire the ability to be typing one thing while listening to another. The machine is only re-actuated a word or two before the typist reaches the end of what she has mentally stored.

The process can, for convenience, be represented graphically like this:

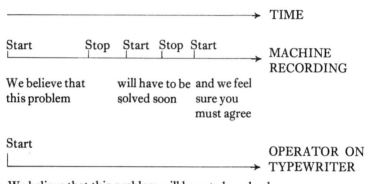

We believe that this problem will have to be solved soon . . .

The development of this skill requires time and a step-by-step approach. Ideally, once the audio-typist begins to type she does not stop until the communication she is engaged on finishes.

Having developed this skill in the early stages it will be a further aim to raise the transcription speed of the student by a transcription training course of the kind described in Chapter 8.

To become good audio-typists, students need just as much in the way of intelligence and knowledge as any other office-skills worker. The idea that audio-typing is a subject suitable for those who would be unsuccessful in learning shorthand is one that will be quickly dismissed by any knowledgeable teacher. The audio-typist needs aural acuity, mental alertness, quick comprehension, speed in typewriting, and a knowledge of words, idioms and sentence structures above the average. Mental storage of words is even more important for the audio-typist than it is for the shorthand-typist because the retention is required for more than twice as long.

Equipment

It is possible to begin audio-typing instruction on a single channel of audio output with a number of built-in stations for the students to plug into with headsets. It has become increasingly clear during the last few years when the subject of audio-typing instruction has been one of experimentation, both in equipment and in teaching methods, that students cannot go far without moving on to individually-controlled transcribers. The lack of homogeneity in response, knowledge and aptitude quickly demands that they must learn as individuals.

The teaching methods and materials can be standardized for the whole group but almost all the practice will need to be under the control of the student. In terms of convenience and cost it is best to provide the same machines and the same system for the whole learning group. To introduce various types of audio machine requiring different kinds of recording media (belt, disc, cassette tapes) and different operating instructions can only complicate the teaching unnecessarily. A student who has learned how to audio-type on one kind of machine will find it comparatively easy to move to a different kind of machine in her actual office work.

Dubbing facilities are readily available today to enable progressive material to be duplicated for each individual learner. Some large commercial manufacturers have special arrangements for the provision of student equipment and these should be investigated before decisions are taken when setting up audio-typing courses.

A full course along the lines of the teaching methods described below is also available.*

Arrangements will need to be made for the regular inspection and maintenance of the machines, and the cassettes or other forms of audio input will need to be carefully preserved in order to keep them free of atmospheric pollution.

When to begin

Grace McNicol in her work, *Teaching Shorthand and Typewriting* (Pitman), said: 'A question to be decided is when to begin the audio-typing course. Should the student be taught typewriting by audio-methods or should, as some authorities think, audio work be left until a competency in typewriting of about 35 words per minute has been reached? On this point there will probably always be more than one opinion. It would not seem to be a matter on which one can be dogmatic.

Really there are two points here. The first is the question whether typewriting itself ought to be taught right from the start by audio methods. The view of the author is that an undeveloped potential for instruction by fully-integrated audio—visual methods, such as video tape,

---

* *Audio-typing: A Progressive Course,* Edith Whicher (Pitman).

exists and that this is likely to be the most fruitful line of future development. The second point is the specific instruction in audio-typing—a
quite different matter. The experience of recent years is that for cost-
effectiveness it is preferable not to begin an audio-typing course until
the students have a safe and confident typing competence of at least 30
wam, higher if possible. Those who begin audio-typing at a lower level
will have their progress hindered as much by their typing inadequacies
as the problems of the new skill.

Nature of the dictation for audio-typing

Most of the matters discussed in Chapter 6 in the section on Dictation
are equally applicable to that intended for the audio-typist. For example,
this dictation should be clearly enunciated in short natural groups of
words with intervals of silence, without hesitations, misreadings, inter-
polations or alterations (particularly not for audio-typists). The words
should be spoken in a natural way but each word should be given its
value without blurring or elision.

The speed of dictation should not much exceed 80 wam; a faster rate
presents the audio-typist with fresh problems of stopping, starting and
playback.

In order to convey the necessary instructions a preliminary dictation
is needed before the actual message begins. Then, during the actual
message, it will be essential to provide the audio-typist with instructions about the exact form of visual representation required. It is strong-
ly urged that the conventions agreed by the Royal Society of Arts should
be those generally adopted as a standardized form of conveying this information and for two good reasons. The first is that for the general
benefit, no matter what system is being used, the conventions need to be
the same so that the audio-typist moving from one job to another or one
department to another does not suddenly find that she is confronted by a
different set of practices. The second is that these conventions have
been very carefully and fully considered, and they represent the clearest
and the most economical way of dealing with the problem. They are
reproduced here:

Audio-typewriting dictation conventions

1. The start of a new paragraph will be indicated by the word
paragraph.

2. Full stops, question marks, colons, semi-colons, dashes and
exclamation marks will be dictated as such.

3. Commas will not be dictated.

4. Parenthesis will be indicated as *open brackets* . . . *close brackets*, and inverted commas as *open double* (or *single*) *quotes* . . . *close quotes.*

5. The solidus will be given as *oblique.*

6. The apostrophe will not be dictated.

7. Initial capitals will not normally be indicated except where there is some particular reason. In cases where capital initials are arbitrary, candidates will not be penalized provided their use of capitals is consistent.

Where indication is necessary, the following method will be used: *initial capital* or *initial capitals*, e.g. '(*initial capitals*) Intermediate Examinations', 'the (*initial capital*) Tower'.

8. The spelling of unusual words will be given after the word has been dictated. The P.O. phonetic alphabet will be used only when dictating single letters which need differentiation, e.g. 'Mr J. C. S. (*for Samuel*) Farmer', 'Mr. P. (*for Peter*) B. (*for Benjamin*) Foulkes (F-O-U-L-K-E-S)'. The P.O. phonetic alphabet is given here:

A for Alfred	**J** for Jack	**S** for Samuel
B for Benjamin	**K** for King	**T** for Tommy
C for Charlie	**L** for London	**U** for Uncle
D for David	**M** for Mary	**V** for Victor
E for Edward	**N** for Nellie	**W** for William
F for Frederick	**O** for Oliver	**X** for X-Ray
G for George	**P** for Peter	**Y** for Yellow
H for Harry	**Q** for Queen	**Z** for Zebra
I for Isaac	**R** for Robert	

9. Instructions for headings will precede the words of the heading, e.g. '(*centred heading, closed capitals, underscored*) MONTHLY SALES RETURNS' or '(*side heading, initial capitals, underscored*) January Sales Figures'.

10. Words to be underscored in a sentence will be dictated and then followed by the instruction *underscore*, e.g. 'This morning's issue of the Daily Telegraph (*underscore Daily Telegraph*)'.

11. The typist should adopt normal practice in typing numbers, dates etc., but where figures or words are specifically required, this will be indicated by an instruction *figures* or *words*, e.g. 'a total of (*figures*) two hundred and fifty' or '(*words*) nineteen hundred and seventy two'.

The twenty-four-hour clock will be dictated as spoken, e.g. 'seventeen hundred hours' (typed as 1700 hrs), 'oh six twenty hours' (typed as 0620 hrs).

12. Pounds sterling will be preceded by the words *pound sign*, e.g.

'(*pound sign*) two point seven five' (£2.75) or '(*pound sign*) oh point five two' (£0.52).

13. Stops will not normally be dictated in abbreviations, but the examiner may require abbreviations to be dictated so as to show whether stops are required or not, e.g. '(*capital letters*) BA', '(*capital letters*) B stop S stop T stop' (B.S.T.).

These conventions do not in fact go as far as many dictators do in modern offices. There will rarely be unanimity of opinion about the extent to which the audio-typist is to be given information on punctuation, the spelling of proper names and difficult words. It is certainly true that, in practice, dictators have found it pays to give more rather than less.

It is important to note also that the need for the addition of this information may unavoidably increase the total amount of dictation by as much as 5–10 per cent. This is a factor not often taken into account when the shorthand/audio comparison is being made. Here, for example, is a piece from an audio-typing examination set by the Scottish Business Education Council. (This passage was compiled before the RSA conventions were published.)

The letter reads:

Dear Mr Robertson (Now a subject heading; centre and use initial capitals) Power Tools (heading ends) When our representative, Mr Green, called on you recently, you expressed interest in our (initial capitals) Power Drills (sentence) Since your trade is mostly with the home handy (hyphen) man, we feel that our (initial capital) Models (figures) D (D David) 500 and D (D David) 720 would be most suitable for your purposes (sentence) We give below the descriptions and recommended retail prices of these models (sentence) On these, you would, of course, receive the customary (figures) 20% mark (hyphen) up. (Indent and display) Model D (figures) 500 (sentence) A sleek all (hyphen) purpose tool (sentence) Drilling speed (figures) 2,600 rpm (revolutions per minute) (sentence) Chuck size (dash. Figures) $\frac{3}{4}''$ (sentence) Drives all attachments (sentence) Price (figures) £6.96 (paragraph) Model D (figures) 720 (sentence) This is a (figure) 2 (hyphen) speed drill (sentence) Chuck size (dash. Figures) $\frac{1}{4}''$ (sentence) The fast speed (dash. Figures) 2,400 rpm (dash) for drilling, sawing or sanding (colon) slow speed (dash. Figures) 900 rpm (dash) for drilling masonry and large holes (sentence) Drives all attachments (sentence) Price (figures) £11.96 (paragraph) There is, of course, a very wide range of attachments for these drills and we are enclosing a booklet giving full details and prices of these (paragraph)

Should you decide to stock our (initial capital) Drills, we will be very pleased to supply you with advertising placards (sentence) I have asked our representative to call on you again in the near future (paragraph) Yours sincerely, Sales Manager. (Indicate that there is an enclosure)

Actual words of the letter: 220

Additional words required by the audio-typing: 76
Percentage increase: 34·6

One cannot help asking the question whether audio-typing is the correct medium for such a letter as this. Would it not have been much clearer and quicker to have written it out in rough manuscript form and handed it to a good typist?—or dictated it to a competent shorthand-typist?

Teaching method

(1) The first step is to familiarize the students with the operation of the machine, so that they will not begin their course with any feelings of apprehension.

(2) In order to concentrate entirely on the listen-and-type skill at the outset, it is best to omit typewriting problems. Single lines of material only are used—the students having been asked to set a 60-stroke line. The original practice will provide a pause at the end of each short sentence to enable the student to return the carriage. Similarly, the early work will be based on very easy words offering no problems at all to average students. For example, we might begin with these sentences:

We shall not be able to come to the meeting next week.
When will you let me have the books to send to my customers?

(3) It is important to cue the early work in order to encourage mental storage and continuous typing. To do this the students are told to listen but not to begin to type until they hear an audio signal (a bleep). After that they go on typing until they come to the end of the sentence and then stop their machine. The sentences are then arranged on the cassette like this:

We shall not be able (bleep)—(interval of 6 seconds)—to come to the meeting—(interval of 6 seconds)—next week (interval of 4 seconds) (stop)
When will you (bleep)—(interval of 4 seconds)—let me have the books—(interval of 6 seconds)—to send to my customers—(Interval of 5 seconds) (question mark)

Time is calculated at 40 wam. That this may be a little fast for some students will not, it will be found, cause any problems in such brief sentences. When two- and three-line sentences are introduced then the intervals should be calculated on 35 wam. It is important to make it clear to the students that they must not stop their machine until they hear the end of the sentence indicated by 'stop', 'question mark' or 'exclamation mark'. Note also that the word groups are very short to begin with, three or four words only.

(4) One lesson of sentences like this is sufficient; in the next two or three lessons longer ones should be used of two or three lines, the punctuation being inserted. The students will still be asked *not* to stop their machines until the end of the sentence is reached, and the cueing bleep will still be included in order to encourage continuous typing. The word groups may be lengthened by a word or two.

(5) After this, students will have a clear idea of what is comprised in the skill and will be ready for the following forward steps:

(*a*) Short paragraphs	Conventions taught	Individual control introduced
(*b*) Longer paragraphs		
(*c*) Short simple letters (no heading, no enclosures, no insets)	Using simplified block layout	All addressee information separately given
(*d*) Progressively longer letters (progressive additions, e.g. headings, references, carbons, enclosures, signatory's designation etc.)		
(*e*) Memorandums		
(*f*) Reports		

(6) The length of the course and the amount of work covered must depend on the goal of the course. If it is to work towards some such qualification as those described in the next section, then a minimum of 30 hours will be needed, a considerable part of which, it will be found, will need to be given to those aspects of transcription that affect accuracy and to preparation to take the passages on the cassettes. There is no reason why, in this training period, some of the pieces should not be read aloud beforehand by the teacher before the preparation is done.

To make use of a prepared course* with its accompanying audio

---

* Edith Whicker, op. cit.

tapes is good sense, since these in no way supplant the teacher. In fact they represent:

(*a*) A substantial saving of effort. The teacher is freed for true teaching in helping, encouraging and observing individuals while the skill is being developed and by discovering and eradicating weaknesses and the formation of wrong habits from the start. More time is available for checking and correcting (very important in audio work) and for maintaining records.

(*b*) The audio programme has been worked out and graded with great care. More care and attention has gone into its compilation than is possible for an individual teacher in a conventional course. Thus time will be used to the best advantage of the students.

(*c*) Well-made cassettes are motivating to the students. During the training period the students ought to be able to rely upon the best audio input if they are to secure the maximum benefit. Cassettes prepared professionally and with care and attention to detail and fidelity of recording and reproduction will be found to be compelling to the students. The essential conditions of learning are met: the students know what to do, why they are doing it, how to do it and what results they are expected to attain.

(7) Further cueing devices that may help to establish the listen-and-type skill firmly in the early stages are:

(*a*) Show the students the first three or four words on chalkboard, pad or OHP transparency. Then ask them to put on their headsets and at a given signal, begin to type. Then at the appropriate point the audio input can be switched on so that the students continue typing without a pause.

(*b*) Occasionally a repetitive method will help to encourage the students to type on continuously, the material being dictated in this fashion:

Please send us some samples—some samples of your latest styles—latest styles in simple summer frocks—summer frocks for the 1976 season.

The total time for this style of dictation must be counted at whatever standard rate (30, 35 or 40 wam) is chosen, ignoring the time taken up by the repetitions. For example, in the illustration quoted there are 17 words, 19 conventional typing words, 95 strokes, and the whole dictation at, say, 40 wam should occupy 27 seconds from 'Please . . .' to '. . . season'.

(*c*) Finally, it is sometimes helpful when the students have begun to 'get the idea' to dictate a whole sentence of 12–20 words before they begin to type at all from the audio input.

(8) Only when the listen-and-type skill is well understood and well established should any more complicated material (either from the viewpoint of content or layout) be introduced. Thereafter the problems of improvement will for the most part be those of transcription training.

8 Teaching Transcription

The need for training in transcription

Typed transcription from shorthand, audio or manuscript is the ultimate stage in the communication chain for the great majority of applications of these skills. It is surprising, therefore, that the subject is not given more attention in office-skills courses. In a survey conducted only a year or two ago by the author, less than 40 per cent of Colleges in Further Education gave a specific allocation of timetable time to the subject and the percentage is certainly no higher in the secondary area. A reflection of this partial neglect may be seen in the figures of a national examining body such as the Royal Society of Arts where the current yearly average of entries is as follows:

Shorthand	90,000
Typewriting	180,000
Shorthand Typists' Certificate	7,000
Audio-Typists' Certificate	4,000

A recent report on the Shorthand-Typewriting examinations of the RSA says: 'The high number of failures in this examination indicate that insufficient time is spent on transcription training' and 'The main cause of failure was the inability of candidates to type back the dictated letter with sufficient accuracy', and on Audio-Typewriting results, the RSA said: 'The main point of failure was spelling . . . often candidates typed nonsense—and were obviously not listening for *sense*.'

Pitman Examinations Institute says: 'In audio-typing the commonest errors are those in spelling and punctuation' and 'Students often fail in shorthand-typing because they do not check their work with sufficient care, either the transcript against the shorthand note, or the typing against the standards of conventional accuracy and presentation that should have been taught.'

One reason for this inadequate attention may well be the exigencies of timetable construction arising from the competing claims of general as well as vocational subjects and the fact that the separate skills are often taught by different staff, and the inability of many students to reach the high standards required for the Shorthand Typists' or Audio Typists' Certificates. Another possible reason is the fact that even today there is no general agreement about the constituents of a course in transcription, and still less about the methods to be employed, the standards to be required and the means of assessment. Yet there is no doubt at all that students who are not given systematic training in the subject will be far less well equipped to cope with the actual situations that will arise in their livelihood earning than those who are.

In 1963 Grace McNicol pointed out that from her own enquiries it was clear that many difficulties in the office could be traced to lack of transcription training. A new skill of look-and-type or listen-and-type has to be learned, along with the necessary correlation of shorthand, audio, typewriting and English skills, plus a number of other important sub-skills. Bright students may 'pick up' the ways of quick, accurate transcription by unstructured practice very much as non-swimmers *may* learn to swim by jumping in at the deep end. But just as most people need to be coached and taught how to swim properly, so do most students who know the basic skills of shorthand and typewriting need to be taught how to transcribe.

What is the skill of transcription?

When we look closely at the operations required in transcription and the elements of knowledge and skill that are called upon, an analysis shows us the following to be basic requirements:

(1) The look-and-type or the listen-and-type skill. Ideally this would mean that the moment the shorthand-typist begins to read and type from her shorthand note, or the moment the audio-typist listens to the first few words and begins to type, the actual typing would then go on without pause to the completion of the message. The uninstructed student will, without preamble, read a few words of her note or tape/cassette, perhaps four or five, and then begin to type these. Then she will stop, go back to the note and take in more words and then type these. Students correctly taught to transcribe will acquire the quite different techniques that are needed from the start and their target or goal will be smooth continuous non-stop typing from words read or heard and assimilated—perhaps 10 or more words ahead of the typing line. Ideally there will be no pauses in the continuous process although, in practice, they will sometimes arise from snags in interpretation or typographical representation, from errors or external interruptions.

(2) An ability to write a complete and readable shorthand note for a period of at least three minutes at 80 wam or above.

(3) An ability to type from copy including figure work and covering all the normal keyboard manipulative operations at a minimum speed of 30 wam.

With reference to these two items, there will be many teachers who will argue that transcription training can begin long before the students can write shorthand or type at these speeds, and they are right of course. Much incidental and small-scale transcription preparation can indeed be done while the students are working their way up to these modest levels. What we are considering in this chapter, however, is full-time teaching units specifically allocated to transcription. To follow such a programme it is best not to begin until the students have reached the kind of standards suggested and for two good reasons. The first is that their lack of command of the contributory skills will interfere positively with their learning and practising of transcription, and the second is that far too much time will be used up in achieving a very low output. Cost effectiveness must be given consideration.

(4) Knowledge of typewriting conventions in matters of layout for letters, memorandums, notices, directives, reports.

(5) Ability to make corrections quickly and effectively.

(6) A reasonable competence in language. It is very hard to define the standards for this with any great precision, although without it the whole process of transcription will break down. For the moment let us state it as a familiarity with the average business vocabulary and with the normal sentence structure, an ability to be able to listen and to read with understanding from material of average difficulty and on subjects within the range of the student's own actual or imagined experience.

Paragraphs (2)–(6) that you have just read represent the basic requirements for beginning training in the skill described in paragraph (1).

Areas of knowledge and skill for development during transcription

As soon as transcription training begins we shall find ourselves obliged to carry existing skills and knowledge further as well as to teach the new basic skill of look-and-type (listen-and-type). These activities will be listed here and then discussed in more detail after we have looked at the realistic office situation.

(*a*) Developing the student's ability to look at shorthand from the transcription viewpoint.

(b) Developing the ability to 'store' words mentally.
(c) Improving the ability to correct errors swiftly and efficiently.
(d) Teaching students how to check and correct their transcript.
(e) Developing their ability to read and assess with speed.
(f) Previewing and preparing transcripts.
(g) Spelling.
(h) Punctuation.
(i) Trap words.
(j) Vocabulary and idiom.
(k) Speed and judgement in making decisions on matters of placement, arrangement, layout and line-ends.

What happens in the real transcription situation?

If our teaching is going to be effective and of maximum value to our
students when they go for their first job, then we need to know in more
than a rough and ready way what goes on in office transcription; this
knowledge will help us frame our own course to the greatest value to the
office beginners. Maximum transfer occurs when the ultimate class conditions, in the problems they present for solution, are close to those
found in the everyday life situation.

More than twenty years ago, Grace McNicol conducted a very careful
survey of office-skills work of nearly 200 employers, whom she asked for
specific comments. In the replies, the following list of items, which they
said were always causing difficulty, appeared in more than 50 per cent of
the answers: inability to punctuate; slow at their work; lacking in
general knowledge; inability to spot errors; poor knowledge of words;
bad spelling; and typewriting inaccuracies.

When the author conducted a similar enquiry in the early 1970s, the
results were much the same. Spelling had moved up the list and a new
element had come in, the implications of which it is not our province
here to discuss: 'Inability or indisposition to work hard.'

We may get a rather different slant on the matter from some research
carried out less than a decade ago by Donald Jester of the Department of
Business Education in De Paul University, Chicago, Illinois, and
published (in the USA) by the South-Western Publishing Company.
The results of this research correspond closely to our own observations
and do not differ very materially from experience in other parts of the
English-speaking world. Rather less than 40 per cent of the total
transcription time of students or untrained junior office-skills workers is
devoted to the actual key-striking and typewriter manipulation; the
remaining 60 per cent is given over to non-typing activities.

Transcription, as we defined it earlier, is a fusion of skills and knowledge but, in addition, it constantly requires problem-solving techniques. This must be the reason why, when the actual typing is taking place, there is a continual recurrence of brief intervals (more than 90 per cent of 30 seconds' duration or less). It follows that transcribers, unless they have years of experience and high expertise in the mechanics of typewriting and in the skill of transcribing, only type at rates just about half as fast as their normal copy speeds. This dictum applies only to that part of the total activity that can be specifically labelled typing. To explain further by an arithmetical example: A transcriber works for 100 minutes, of which 40 minutes is typing. If her straight-copy speed is, say, 50 wam, she will achieve 25 wam for 40 minutes = 1,000 words. If we measured transcription speed, as we ought, over the whole operation, she would achieve 25 wam for 100 minutes, i.e. 2,500 words. For the inexperienced learner-transcriber, something less than this, i.e. 20 wam = 2,000 word, is the practicable goal. So the gap between potential and performance in the untrained transcriber is 1,000 words in 100 minutes. Nevertheless, there is of course a significant correlation between straight copying speeds and typing speeds during transcription.

What are the chief causes of this undesirable state of affairs? A first-class transcriber ought to be able to manage—and does in fact, as we have discovered from our research—to achieve overall transcription speed of half copy speed, or even more; this is the gap that needs to be closed. What are the obstacles in the way?

Extrapolating from Donald Jester's own work and from our own observations and couching this in a simplified form, the total time is parcelled out like this:

Analysis of transcription time

Activity	Unit
Typing	40
Erasures	14
Proof-reading (checking)	8
Shorthand or audio puzzles	6
Reading (or listening) for meaning	4
Preparing	4
Spelling problems	6
Supplying letter details	3
Punctuation problems	5

All these categories will be clear enough, with the possible exception of 'reading for meaning'. There are two elements here: first, stopping to read or to listen ahead in order to know what to type; and, second, making sure of the right words, as distinct from spellings (e.g. *effect* or *affect*? Is it *relevant* or *revelant*?).

This is where the time goes, and we need to have these factors before us when planning our teaching of this composite skill.

(1) The fact of continual breaks is not only to be attributed to the difficulties listed. It springs also from a lack of correct training to achieve the look-and-type and listen-and-type techniques, which do not happen naturally but have to be coached and taught.

(2) The time taken for correction looms large in the total package. Our own records show that when a girl sets out to transcribe from a shorthand note or an audio input her error rate rises sharply; often it doubles. Part of this is no doubt attributable to the change in the stimulus medium—from plain, well-laid-out copy to a stimulus at one remove, namely a set of symbols or a transient aural impression. Therefore, we ought to do everything we can do to improve that input medium. The student shorthand-typist is instructed in the improvement and clarification of her note so that potential error is reduced; but there is little we can do for the audio-typist who has to put up with what she can get, but in the training period we can ensure that what she is given sets a standard for what she ought to demand when she is out at work.

Another part of this rise in error is certainly due to dissipated concentration. The transcriber has a lot of things to think about—her layout, placement, line-ends, spelling, doubts about meanings of words and so on—and all these distract her and make her error-prone. What we have to do is to minimize these disturbing elements by giving her, through familiarity with her work, the confidence she lacks.

Errors are of two kinds—there are those you know you have made as soon as you have made them, and these of course are corrected on the spot; then there are those that you do not know you have made until you come to your proof-reading or checking stage—which you may miss even then. It is interesting to note that in the first kind all the time goes on correction; in the second kind, the time taken to discover the error is dominant and the time for correction secondary. It is clear from this that it is necessary to familiarize the learner with proof-reading so that she approaches it systematically, and knows what she is looking for.

Finally, there is the correction itself, and the attitude of mind that has to be adopted when error occurs. We have all had the experience of making a mistake and then almost at once making another as a result of the shock of making the first, and a third one for good measure while we recover our equilibrium. We need training to accept the inevitability of error and to preserve our equanimity. By the same token we need training, almost like an army drill by numbers, to go into our expert error-correction routine—fast, orderly and well executed.

By proper instruction this inflated consumption of time on erasure can be brought down to less than half.

No doubt the figure given here would be lower today as a result of the very rapid introduction during the last few years of various chemico-mechanical means of correcting typewriting mistakes quickly.

(3) The fact that eight units of time in transcription is devoted to proof-reading is not to be deplored as it is vital to the whole process.

Still there is little doubt that systematic teaching will greatly assist the learner, and reduce the time necessarily devoted to it. Many treat it as an incidental activity, an art that is acquired rather than learned, but it seems that this is not enough. In teaching proof-reading we can identify separate stages—not necessarily sequential—but used at various times until the final goal is safely attained. For the purpose, *ad hoc* material is necessary as well as the actual transcription work of the learner.

The matter will be dealt with more fully below.

(4) Six units of the transcriber's time is taken up with dealing with problems of input: they cannot read their shorthand notes or they cannot make sense of what they hear on the audio tape. For the audio-typist, one can only have sympathy since she has no way open to her of controlling or improving the input. For the shorthand-typist and secretary there is much that can be done and one ought not to be spending five minutes in every hour sorting out shorthand puzzles.

In teaching transcription we have to give the dictation at a cruising speed—the speed at which the learner feels under no stress as she makes her note. Given that condition, we then have to devote time and attention to the analysis of the note, and this can only be done effectively on an individual basis.

The best way of discovering the shorthand problems is to request an oral read-back by two or three of the learners immediately the original dictation is completed. Then, as the reading proceeds, make a note of every stop or hesitancy or mis-reading and when the reading is completed collect the raw notes and scrutinize them; in the next instruction period they can be returned to the writers with a positive and helpful critique. In this fashion every student may have her notes for transcription looked at closely once every seven or eight days.

This work has to be supplemented by specific instruction in how to improve a shorthand note before transcription begins. Whether during learning or in the office, a transcriber ought not to begin without this vital read-through. The time spent on it (which is usually too short) will be more than recovered by a smooth, non-stop transcription based on confidence and therefore less likely to contain errors.

(5) Four units of total transcription time are taken up with reading for meaning and this involves: (*a*) stopping to read or listen ahead in order to know what to type, and (*b*) to make sure of the right words. Ideally it ought to be possible to save nearly all of this time: if the read-through after dictation has been properly done, and if the learner has been correctly taught the look-and-type or listen-and-type technique, then the necessity of stopping ought very rarely to arise. A first-class transcriber is reading ahead anything from three to fifteen words while actually typing and at the same time interpreting the meaning of what she is just about to type. We have a very good knowledge from years of experience of the words, the idioms, the structures that are most likely to cause this kind of hold-up and these should be taught systematically as part of the organized course of transcription training. For example, looking at it from both ends of the scale, we ought to begin with words such as *to, there, its, off, already,* and at the end of the course be dealing with words such as *immigrant, censure, ware, elusive* and *illusory.* No course can cover every possibility of hold-up in the vast resources of the English language. Occasionally there are bound to be unusual words or idioms quite unknown to the transcriber, but in the business context these will be rare enough if we, as teachers, have done our work properly.

(6) Preparing to transcribe takes another four units of the total time. Where this involves the assembling of the materials for the job—the paper, the carbons, eraser, envelopes, correspondence, files, references—and where it involves the read-through then, of course, it is time well spent and indispensable to the total operation. What we need to do is to ensure that the performance of preparation is organized and systematic. Herein lies the only hope of time-saving in this necessary activity.

(7) It is no surprise to find that spelling problems occupy another six units of the total transcription time. In his survey, Donald Jester found that this was the foremost English problem and he concludes by saying: 'it is beyond the scope of this study to predict an expected frequency for the occurrence of spelling problems.' No doubt he is right, although there is one effective answer to the problem, but no course of training will eliminate every spelling problem for every transcriber. Yet as those who have studied the article 'Spelling: How to Trap an Old Bugbear',

Office Skills (March 1972) will know, adopting the methods detailed there will totally eliminate at least 75 per cent of these problems. So systematic attention to spelling—using these methods—is a vital part of every course of transcription training. A transcriber who has gone through such a course will not have more than two such problems in every three 200-word business communications. Worked out in terms of total time, the spelling-problem element in transcription can be reduced to less than two units.

(8) Letter details occupy three units of time. The items included under this heading were the details and placement of inside address, of signature elements, of complimentary closure, salutation, references, date, enclosure notations, copy distribution, continuation-sheet details. In addition, they included checking figures and amounts incorporated in the texts to be transcribed.

All this is, of course, very important and indispensable. However, it is clear from our own research (*Memo Key*, December 1969) and that carried out by the Civil Service Department that if only the standard layout in open-punctuated fully-blocked style were universally adopted, very considerable savings would be effected.

(9) The last of the time-consuming non-typing activities that still runs away with five units of transcription time is in solving punctuation problems. Donald Jester found, rather surprisingly, that as a means of separating two independent clauses in the one sentence the comma was the most bothersome.

It is no good imagining that the problem can be solved by anything less than systematic coverage of the kind of punctuation required in business, or by anything less than an understanding of the principles that underlie it. Punctuation taught on the basis of 'there's a pause there, so put in a comma or a semi-colon' is worse than useless. The fact that students come to us with far less than adequate knowledge in this area is just unfortunate: it is our task to put that right.*

Now we are ready to take a closer look at those items listed in the section on *Areas of knowledge and skill for development during transcription.* The same letter identification will be used as in that section.

(a) Shorthand from the transcription viewpoint

It is at this stage that the student will begin to appreciate the value of inserting a helpful vowel, diphthong or double vowel (diphone) in order to give instant readability. Initial vowels are particularly helpful, unless their presence is otherwise shown by the nature of the shorthand

---

* See *Business Punctuation* (Pitman).

outline. Here too, inserting the full stops, indicating capital letters, making sure a safe figure writing, all contribute to the desired goal of unhesitating read-back and transcription.

We need also to teach our students how to relate a page or a half-page of her notes with the appearance of the transcribed piece on an A4 or A5 or two-thirds A4 sheet. We need to give the student practice from time to time in relating the number of words of her note to their appearance in pica or elite on these different sizes of paper.

For a 300-word piece, the student ought to have three minutes for the necessary 'run-through'. Time spent on preparing a note before typing begins will result in a speedier and more efficient transcription. The same is true for the audio-typist—not in the sense that she should listen to the whole message before beginning work on it, although that is, in fact, sometimes done, but in carefully attending to all the preliminaries and assimilating the information given so that when she actually begins transcribing she is confident about what she is doing.

During this 'run-through' the shorthand-typist inserts punctuation, corrects outlines where these cause momentary hold-ups, establishes the paragraphing if it has not already been given, makes sure of capital letters, hyphens, dashes, apostrophes, proper nouns, adjectives, quotes, headings and sub-headings (if needed).

(b) Mental storage
Means of developing the ability to carry words mentally have already been discussed earlier in this work. During the transcription periods one or two minutes devoted to direct dictation on to the typewriter will also be an effective method. For example, early in the course you can dictate once only, five sentences having 4, 6, 8, 10, 12 words, as in:

We shall telephone tomorrow

Please send us your current catalogue

We are hoping to have more information soon

We have been unable to trace the order in our files

We do not yet know why there has been this long delay

and tell the students not to begin until you give the word, 'Type', after a pause of two or three seconds at the end of each sentence. Later in the course the 4- and 6-word sentences can be dropped and 14-, 16- and even 18-word sentences added.

(c) Error correction
Correcting errors, as we have suggested earlier, must be learned as a

systematic drill and we can begin by associating the verbal instructions with the actions. After a while the cues of verbal instruction can be dropped, once the students have a confident built-in response to error. Again it is of value in the early stages to incorporate specific one- or two-minute drills for this purpose. A line with a deliberate mistake can be written on chalkboard or OHP transparency (wrong letter, transposition, omitted letter, wrong spelling, wrong word—*principle* for *principal*, for example—are types to be used). The mistake is first identified, then the students type the line with it in and wait; when they are all ready, the signal is given for the correction to be made. The process should be timed by stopwatch, only the fastest times being recorded. Watch the slower ones in particular in order to help them improve their technique. Allow any appropriate method of correction.

(d) Checking and correcting

We loosely use proof-reading as a term to describe the activity of checking and correcting. It is a specialized publishing activity requiring a wider knowledge and ability than typists will ordinarily be called upon to possess. Checking and correcting, on the other hand, is an indispensable element in the transcription process. The reasons why it is not usually well done are that students are not sure about what they are looking for, and have often had no graded practice in it. The range of possible errors is wide: they may be typographical, they may arise from wrong spelling or omitted or incorrect punctuation, from mis-transcription resulting from a failure of understanding, or from typing one word for another which resembles it.

In teaching transcription there are two ways of going about the problem. The first is incidental to the student's own transcripts but it is very important. Sometimes students may be called upon to check their own transcript from a model which could well be an OHP transparency or a printed or duplicated page; they should be penalized not for the errors they make but for those they fail to locate in their own work. Alternatively, the teacher may collect four or five transcripts in each period and indicate to the students where the errors are—and in the early stages their nature—by a solidus against the line where they occur. A simple code for such marking is quickly learned and understood: **T** = typing error; **P** = punctuation error, to which we may add **A** = apostrophe error and **H** = hyphenation error; **S** = spelling error; **W** = wrong word (either a mis-transcription or a word mistaken for another one like it); **E** = English error, as singular for plural, or a grammatical mistake like the wrong tense of a verb; omission with a caret showing where this is located. Later on it will be sufficient to use a solidus only, leaving it to the students to find out what is wrong.

Time must then be found to discuss these points with each student individually. Marking without oral comment is, from the student's viewpoint, a waste of time.

The second way of going about the problem is a systematic *ad hoc* approach in which the students are called upon to learn how to check and correct step by step. The stages by which this may be done are now described.

(1) A direct comparison in two vertical columns of one phrase or group of words with another, the student being asked just to write in **S** or **D** according to whether the two items to be compared are the 'same' or 'different'. Here is a brief example of the kind of exercise that might be used:

			S	D
1	Dupont, Brown & Co. Ltd.	Dupont, Brown & Co Ltd.		
2	Send 18,436 copies today	Send 18,436 copies to-day		
3	Use 2/3 A4 paper w e f now	Use 2/3 A4 paper w e f now		
4	Freeman Hardy Willis	Freeman Hardy Willes		
5	Please refer to our Order A/21/10964	Please refer to our Order A/21/10694		
6	Mr A L Featherstonehaugh MA Dip Ed	Mr A L Featherstonehaugh MA Dip Ed		
7	Call into see us on 12th May	Call in to see us on 12th May		
8	Unsuccessful candidates must re-enter	Unsuccessful candidates must re-enter		
9	Pakistan rupee – Rs. 11.43 = £1	Pakistan rupee – Rs. 11.43 £1		
10	The NCOs' canteen is in Trinity Street	The NCOs' canteen in is Trinity Street		
11	What's this? An Assyrian palimpsest?	What's this? An Assyrian palimpsest?		
12	Put each specimen into a seperate bag	Put each specimen into a separate bag		
13	141-146 Chrichton Street CIRENCESTER	141-146 Chrichton Street CIRENCESTER		
14	Total imports $ 5,083,853,546	Total imports $ 5,083,853,546		
15	Total exports $ 3,890,684,596	Total exports $ 3,890,684,569		

16	'NO SMOKING' notices are exhibited	'NO SMOKING notices are exhibited	
17	Jane Austen's novel _Emma_ is the apogee.	Jane Austen's novel _Emma_ is the apogee.	
18	V. infra op. cit. Pp. 100, 110.	V. infra op. cit. Pp 100,110.	
19	Vice Admiral (Vice-Adm.).	Vice-Admiral (Vice-Adm.).	
20	Albion House 34 Leadenhall St EC3	Albion House 34 Leadenhall St EC3.	

(2) A passage in which there are a given number of errors of one particular type such as: spelling, wrong words, typing, punctuation, English. These are indicated in the script by a marginal solidus against the line where they occur. The student is called upon to locate the errors and, where appropriate, to re-type correctly. A time limit is set for the operation.

(3) The next stage is to combine two of these varieties, still indicating by solidus and identifying letter to show the nature of the mistake.

(4) The next stage is to repeat this kind of exercise but restrict the indications to unlettered soliduses.

(5) The final stage is to give the piece and state the number of errors, but without indicating where they occur.

Clearly, the drills will need to be composed so as to include only those errors which the students have already covered in their transcription course.

Students trained in this step-by-step progressive way will reach the end of their course with a much sharper eye for mistakes, and more confidence in going about the necessary work of checking while the typescript is still in the machine.

(e) Reading and assessing

The ability to recognize and absorb the sense of a passage quickly, whether in the form of a shorthand note, a manuscript or an audio cassette, depends on the extent of one's vocabulary and knowledge of the structures of the English sentence, on general and other knowledge according to the sense of the passage. Students whose shorthand reading and typing-copy material is confined to narrow subject limits like simple business letters and company reports, will be good transcribers only within those narrow limits. Therefore, a fairly broad selection of reading on a range of topics of current interest and importance is an essential part of a transcription course.

Practice in visual comprehension ought not to be omitted. There are two particular aspects of it that are relevant to the office situation. The first is speed of reading (which may vary all the way from 150–800 wam) and we can bring about improvement in this area by specific and guided practice.* The second is reading for a purpose, for example to briefly summarize the main argument, or to select from the passage particular items that are required, or to find out by inference what conclusions may be drawn or to provide the answers to specific questions known in advance. This is the kind of reading that is often required of office-skills workers after they have had some experience and gained some responsibility. In any case, fast and concentrated reading for sense is going to be of value to them in their transcription.

(f) Previewing and preparing transcripts
When planning a transcription course, the work to be done may be regarded as falling into two parts. The first is the progressive build-up of the transcription skill; the second is the development of all the ancillary skills, some of which we are now discussing.

Much of the work in developing the transcription skill will require preparation. Even when students have acquired a reasonable competence they will not be able to tackle successfully a piece that comes entirely fresh to them because they will still lack the kinds of knowledge and sub-skills required to achieve it. Only when they are at the end of the course can we let them 'go it alone' as they will have to do in their job. At stages along the way we shall set these 'unseens' as a challenge to them and as a motivation exercise, ensuring by careful composition that they are able to cope with the difficulties.

As in shorthand-speed development, the preparation can vary all the way from a few outlines, a few words and hints, up to a full-scale and comprehensive presentation of all the script, all the shorthand, all the aural—together with vocabulary, idiom, spelling, paragraphing, punctuation, shorthand outlines and phrases, aural difficulties. How far to follow this line must depend upon class attainment and the teacher's judgement of how much is necessary for success.†

---

* *Quicker Reading*, Harry Bayley (Pitman).

† In the author's text *Transcription Training* (Pitman), each of the thirty units contains the full text of the Practice Piece for transcription and notes on it. It is left to the teacher how far to make use of this, and how much of the shorthand to provide for the students.

Preparation along the lines suggested above, some discussion of length, placement, and verbal, aural, or shorthand problems is necessary for most of the work throughout most of the course.

Preview may be interpreted as a preliminary look at a piece ultimately to be transcribed from shorthand or from audio cassette, either by a study of:

(i) All the shorthand correctly written in copperplate or facsimile, side by side with all the printed or typed script fully and correctly punctuated; or

(ii) All the printed or typed script side by side with read-through aloud followed by a read-through without reference to the script.

In one sense the preview can be the ultimate in preparation. Undoubtedly, it is a most useful way of building up transcription skill especially if the passages are well chosen.

A useful modification of the preview, developed and very successfully used by Grace McNicol, is to take a piece chosen for its interest and English and/or shorthand knowledge, of about 200–300 words and use it in the following manner:

(i) A copy of the shorthand in fully punctuated facsimile is given to each student. The piece is read and points of transcription are discussed.

(ii) A week later the shorthand is given to the students again, only this time unpunctuated apart from the full stops. The students are asked to re-read it silently but they are allowed to ask questions. At the end of a given time (say 3–4 minutes) they are then required to do a timed transcript of the whole piece. This will generally take 10 minutes or less.

(g) Spelling

A full treatment of spelling from the viewpoint of office work is given in the article referred to above entitled 'Spelling: How to Trap an Old Bugbear', *Office Skills* (March 1972). Spelling has been somewhat neglected in schools during the past decade but it has a direct and obvious importance in transcription, and since spelling standards are well known to be low it is essential to improve students' spelling during the course. There are two possible approaches and both of them, if systematically followed through, will produce substantial and measurable improvements.

The first approach is the individual and incidental. A check is kept on the actual errors made by individuals in their transcription work and from time to time these words are revised with those concerned.

The second approach is the formal one which, if followed up with persistence and regularity, will get rid of 80 per cent or more of all errors. The 235 most commonly misspelled words will be found listed alphabetically in the Appendix. If 8 or 10 of these are presented in each week of a course and learned by the students to the point of 100 per cent success (the only worthwhile standard for this work) the whole group can be learned by the end of the course.

Since spelling is largely a visual matter it is best to present the words in three or four different ways: handwritten, typescript capital letters, typescript lower-case letters, printed lower-case letters. The words are shown correctly used in context and underscored. Students copy these sentences which are then dictated for shorthand or for audio transcript and the results of transcription checked. At this point, the author has found the best procedure is to note on the chalkboard the number of errors arising for each word. If one or two words have been correctly typed by all members of the group, then these may be omitted. From this we may get a result:

separate	6	benefited	3
occasion	2	unnecessary	5
privilege	4	omitted	1
accommodation	9	secretarial	2

These words are then re-dictated in the context of new sentences and on the next check we may well find that *occasion, omitted, secretarial* and *benefited* now give rise to no error. We continue the process until every individual in the class (working as a class) has got every spelling right.

At the end of each week or fortnight, a review test will be necessary to consolidate the improvement in spelling.

It will be noted that the list given for this kind of practice consists entirely of words in general and regular use in everyday contexts. One may be forgiven for getting words like *iridescent* or *sacrilegious* wrong, but not for mistakes in words like *separate* or *necessary*.

We cannot cover the whole field of idiosyncratic English orthography but we can be sure of getting the common words right all the time.

(h) Punctuation
Students generally have little knowledge of punctuation and no liking

for it, the reason being that it is often given only a perfunctory attention. Not surprisingly, weakness in punctuation is always among the complaints of employers about the inadequacies of their office-skills workers.

To the communications operative, punctuation is highly important and unless the topic is properly dealt with the weaknesses will remain.

It is true that there is an area of punctuation that is debatable—even controversial sometimes—but that area is small compared with the large area within which there is agreement.

Punctuation appropriate for business communications can be successfully taught by teachers who understand syntax and it can be successfully learned by students of average ability. The main point is that it cannot be taught in a vacuum; it has to be taught through syntactical structure, and only when the students understand the structure can they get the punctuation right. This means that there is a nettle to be grasped right at the outset of teaching punctuation and that is the concept of the sentence itself. One of the commonest failings of uninstructed students is in writing a comma (or nothing at all) where a full stop should be, or less frequently writing a full stop before the sentence has come to an end.

Now the concept of the sentence is a subtle and difficult one and linguists are still arguing it out. Here, for instance, is the definition of a sentence as given by Leonard Bloomfield in his book *Language* (ULP): 'an independent linguistic form, not included by virtue of any grammatical construction in any larger linguistic form.' John Lyons in his book *Introduction to Theoretical Linguistics* (CUP)—a tough 'introduction' indeed but one which every teacher should study—gives this definition: 'The sentence is the maximum unit of grammatical analysis: that is, it is the largest unit that the linguist recognizes in order to account for the distributional relations of selection and exclusion that are found to hold in the language he is describing.'

Clearly, even to understand such concepts we need a background of linguistic study; but luckily we can make do quite satisfactorily with a definition much less subtle and profound. Something like this perhaps: 'A sentence is an orderly sequence of words that comprises a whole idea and contains at least one finite verb.' Then we have to make quite sure that the student understands exactly what a finite verb is and is given the necessary practice to establish unerring recognition. From this it is an easy step to the sentence–clause–phrase–word idea.

Once past this initial hurdle, the most difficult part is over; all the rest follows on step-by-step without great difficulty. The sequence of step-by-step knowledge of structure and the punctuation (or absence of punctuation) that relates to it that the author has found to be the most practicable is as follows:

1. Placing of full stops.
2. Use of capital letters, question marks, exclamation marks.
3. Commas in series, in co-ordinating clauses, after adverbial clauses, in appositions, in non-defining relative clauses, in participial phrases, to mark off introductory or linking phrases.
4. The treatment of acronyms and abbreviations.
5. Punctuation used in sub-headings.
6. Colons to introduce sub-headed material or speech.
7. Semi-colons to mark off contrasts, antitheses or logically sequential clauses.
8. Quotes, dashes, apostrophes.
9. Hyphenation.

The underlying principles that we have by repetition to get our students to understand are:

(i) Punctuation is only needed as an aid to understanding and ease of reading.

(ii) The minimum of punctuation consonant with instant comprehension is the aim in business communication.

(iii) The rules taught are those generally accepted in modern practice by writers, editors and publishers.

(iv) If any punctuation is still uncertain (as, for example, whether to separate, hyphenate, or write 'solid') then we tell the student so and the reasons why, and we argue for the acceptance of this or that punctuation on the basis of the principles already given.

For the manner in which this necessary teaching may be presented and the practice given, the reader is referred to *Transcription Training* (op. cit.) and to *Business Punctuation* (Pitman).

(i) Trap words

The English language is full of traps for the unwary, the most persistent cause of error in the work of office-skills employees being the considerable number of quite common words that have a close enough resemblance to one another to give rise to confusion. This confusion may arise from the closeness in appearance (of, off; lightning, lightening) or from a difficulty in sorting out the meaning (infer, imply; effect, affect). It seems that incidental treatment of such words as they arise in the material used for transcription is not of itself enough. A transcription course will need to incorporate specific treatment of at least 100 or so of the most troublesome of these words. From what we know of learning it is unwise to treat two or three of these similar words at the same time; the result may merely be to introduce confusion where there was none before.

It is preferable, for example, to treat *effect* by itself, showing it in context sentences in both of its main uses: as a noun meaning 'result, consequence' and as a verb meaning 'to bring about, to complete successfully'. Then a little later test the student on the knowledge acquired, and only when this word is thoroughly learned and understood, introduce a week or two later the word *affect* in the same way. In the early learning, students will generally need the support of cues (e.g. the required words given in consonantal outline; a list of words for choice or for insertion *without* possible confusions); later, they will need to show their grasp of the words by using them in sentences of their own composition.

Such work may not be the most enthralling in the world, yet interest in it can be maintained by these systematic methods.

(j) Vocabulary

A course in transcription is demanding of time. Although it is soon apparent that gaps in the students' knowledge of words and idioms is a main cause for slowness or inaccuracy in transcription, there is really not much that can be done, except incidentally, to make good such a weakness. The time for a systematic attempt to improve the recognition and recall vocabulary of the students is not available. What we have to do is to ensure that in preparing a piece for transcription all the students know the words and idioms in the piece. We can also perhaps make an attempt to build up a more specifically business vocabulary and we can certainly encourage students by constant precept and personal example to use a dictionary, and in particular to teach them how to use it.

A not untypical student reaction to a question about a word is to say: 'I know what it means but I can't really express it (explain it, say it, etc.)'. If a student cannot say what a word or expression means, that student does not know what it means.

Much can be done in this field by encouraging students to read good books. This is not to be interpreted as encouraging students only to read the classics of our literature; there are also fine modern books, not only novels but documentaries, that are very well written and more likely to establish an immediate rapport with the student's world. The Penguin and other paperback lists are a treasure store for such works.

In my own teaching I made it a practice once a week to read a passage of 500–1,000 words aloud, carefully chosen for its intrinsic and self-contained interest to my students. I read it as best I knew how. Then I wrote on the chalkboard the name of the author and the book, nothing else. If no questions came, that was the end of it; if questions were asked—and they were, more often than not—I would cheerfully devote 10 or 15 minutes to answering them, discussing with the students and broadening the picture. It might finish up with half a dozen other recommendations. My philosophy was that if I could only interest one or two students each week to the point where they would actually get the book and read it, then what I had done was justified.

(k) Speed and judgement

The production of a good transcript involves the student in making decisions. As in typewriting, the sooner we can allow them to make their own, and thus approach the office situation, yet retain the benefit of the teacher's comment and guidance, the better. What are these decisions? They vary from the elementary to the quite complex: What size of paper? What margins? What placement on the paper? How many copies, if any? What address and signatory details, and so on? What kind of display (as in a notice, a report or a directive)? Have I left any uncorrected mistake? Is this good enough—could I have done it better in the same length of time?

After a piece for transcription has been prepared with greater or less detail, according to the teacher's judgement of what is needed, and the students have completed the job, then it is good practice to exhibit, preferably by an OHP transparency or by a duplicated copy, a model for them to judge their own results by—not just its accuracy, correctness and completeness, but also its appearance, its ease of reading and understanding, its fitness for its purpose.

The decisions that students and office-skills workers often make unconsciously have to be brought to the forefront of their minds and, if necessary, explained.

Transcription course

From the discussion of transcription training up to this point, the table given below that outlines a course in the subject will be self-explanatory. How much time should be devoted to it must depend on how much is available within the terms of reference; it is hardly possible to have too much, and all too easy to have too little.

It may be helpful at this point to visualize a typical 45-minute lesson and how it may proceed.

Transcription

Time Material	Length	Method
Short easy plain matter items sentences paragraphs 5 hours?	1–3 mins (20–80 words)	Some 'plate'. Some facsimile. Then copied note. Then own note from dictation.
Letters 30 hours?*	5–10 mins (80–150 words)	Preview. Prepare copy. Free note. Standard OP/FB layout. Introduce carbons, corrections.
Letters Memorandums Notices Directives Reports 30 hours?*	5–15 mins (80–250 words)	Preview. Prepare copy. Free note. Standard layout. Introduce envelopes, enclosures, circulated copies, continuation sheets.
Groups of items 15 hours?*	10–30 mins (80–500 words)	Preview. Less preparation. Free note.

Ancillaries

Type	Content	Method
Spelling	Sentences. Short continuous pieces.	Copy. Then shorthand note. Transcribe Test Items.

Notes: (i) *In every second or third lesson, introduce a short unprepared item for 'free' dictation and immediate transcription. (ii) All the ancillary items are carried forward progressively and simultaneously as integral parts of every transcription period.

Ancillaries (contd.)

Type	Content	Method
Punctuation	Sentences. Short continuous pieces.	Copy. Then shorthand note. Transcribe Test Items.
Trap Words	Sentences.	Copy. Then shorthand note. Transcribe Test Items.
Proof-reading	*Ad hoc* content (i) S & P (ii) Typographical (iii) Words First located by line, then by number. Then mixed. Student's own material simultaneously.	Locating and correcting error. Erasure drills.
Words, Idioms Structures	As they occur in the material.	Incidental during preparation. Test items every 4 or 5 weeks.

Our lesson plan says:

(1) Students' warm-up transcription.

(2) Teach: separate, accommodation, believed, unnecessary, referred. Exercise from shorthand (or audio).

(3) Teach: apostrophes for singular possession.

(4) Read 150 words of a notice. Check spellings, punctuation, words and expressions.
Re-read from shorthand.

(5) Dictate at 80 wam. Allow 2 minutes note improvement.

(6) Teach: storey, cite, whose, practice, prophecy(ies).
Dictate illustrative sentences.

(7) Students to transcribe notice ((4) above) from their own note (or audio cassette). Total time (with one copy): 6 minutes.

Collect students' exercises for checking and the remainder for re-distribution next period.

(8) Dictate 80 words unseen at 70 wam. Two-minute read-through. Time completed transcript for each student in minutes and seconds. Allot transcript speed.

(9) Redictate spellings.

This, hopefully, will be a packed, non-stop, hard-working period, yet full of variety and interest.

The warm-up transcription will consist, for shorthand-typists, of a 20-word sentence in vocalized shorthand to be transcribed from the chalkboard; for audio typists it will consist of a 20-word sentence in which half the words are given only in suggestive consonantal outline.

In the teaching of spellings, the students will see the words in various presentations and will copy them; they will read them in context. Then the sentences will be dictated for a shorthand note and transcribed from that note and checked. All students will be required to get every word right.

The material for preparation will be presented first in correct typescript, then in shorthand, with such notes as may be needed given in between. After this preparation and before the actual transcript we interpose instruction with dictated examples on some of the trap words.

When it comes to the actual transcription it is important for students to be aware of the pressure of time. We can find out how much they can get done and how accurately within a specified time or, alternatively, require them to indicate their own time when they have completed the particular exercise and are satisfied that they have corrected it as far as they can.

Similarly, the manner in which the work is to be assessed is especially important in transcription training, and this is discussed fully in Chapter 11. Briefly it may be said that in transcription, checking is of paramount importance: sometimes it must depend on the students' own efforts; sometimes it must be done by the teacher. In any case it is essential that the student identifies and understands each error, and according to its nature, does remedial work on it. Moreover, the assessment must be based on the quality and accuracy of the transcript, with regard to extent and the speed of execution.

9 Marking

Teachers of office skills have to undertake the marking of work done by their students, whose written output in the form of shorthand notes, typed exercises, transcripts from shorthand, audio or manuscript input is considerable. Moreover, the longer the course, the greater the volume of the output.

Some problems that have to be considered therefore are these: What is the purpose of marking? How much of the students' work should be marked? What methods should be adopted?

Fortunately, for the most part, the subjects we teach lend themselves to highly objective testing, and because the students' work constantly supplies us with information about their abilities, weaknesses and relative and absolute attainments, the actual number of tests needed is few.

The marking of work must be to the benefit of the student, otherwise it is not worth doing. Therefore we must find ways of ensuring that the student does learn from our marking, if we can see good reasons why it should be done in the first place!

There is a second aim that is of equal importance: only through marking can we establish and maintain those standards of work that we decide are acceptable. Students will work down to our standards if we pitch them too low, and they will, equally, work up to our standards if we insist from the beginning upon their being high. The author's experience is that average students will respond well to discipline in the matter of acceptable standards.

To set oneself to study closely and to mark in detail every single line of work produced by our students is, for most of us, an impossible and unproductive task. A most important part of our teaching of office skills lies in making our students self-reliant in matters of checking and correcting; at the end of their course they should have learned how to look at their own output with an informed and self-critical eye, reasonably confident of their ability when they are 'on their own' of doing things in the right way and putting right their own inevitable mistakes (which will, we hope, be as few as possible).

Since we are unlikely, except in the very early stages, to be able to mark everything that the students produce, what reasonable solutions to the problem can be found?

There are two approaches that, when used together, the author has found to be of value. The first is to mark everything produced in a particular lesson by four or five students; the second is to collect and mark one single piece of each student's work done in a particular lesson. By this means, individuals receive concentrated specialized attention at regular intervals, and all get some of their work checked all the time. The work selected to be marked must first warrant that amount of attention.

Students have a right to expect that when a piece of work is submitted, then it should be fully and conscientiously marked. Conversely, as teachers we have the right and the duty to expect that when the marked work is returned, it should be conscientiously scrutinized, understood, and where necessary the correct remedial work done by way of correction. What must not happen is that the student merely glances at the returned work, notes the numerical mark (if one has been given) and then merely files it, or worse still, throws it away.

For this reason time must be found first to comment in a general way, constructively if possible, on the returned work, and then later to speak to each individual about their own exercises and what may be derived from them to help them for the future.

The adoption of a marking code will save much time, avoid defacing an exercise to the point where a student will be discouraged or frustrated by the sheer quantity of correction that meets his eye, and enable a constructive rather than a destructive approach to be adopted when going through the marked work.

Here are some suggestions of the kind of marks that might be adopted. The author has made use of all these and students quickly grasp their meaning.

u c	upper case; capital letters
l c	lower case; small, not capital letters
w	wrong word
⋀ or ◯	omission; if with a figure, the number of words omitted
in⌣to	write solid as one word
may⌐be	separate into two words

⟨transpose symbol⟩	transpose
S	spelling wrong
E	English incorrect (e.g. a wrong agreement, wrong tense, singular for plural, etc.)
A	apostrophe (omitted or wrongly placed)
#1	space (with figure indicating how many spaces)
H	hyphenate
P	punctuation is incorrect or omitted
⊙	full stop
NP	new paragraph
⌒	run on without a break
No A	no apostrophe

From time to time it is useful to make the marking selective as, for example, confining it to spelling and punctuation only. It is important then that the students should clearly understand what the marking does, and does not, signify.

Sometimes too, especially when the students begin to develop an awareness of the standards of accuracy required and the types of mistake that can arise, it is constructive to mark only with marginal solidusess to show where the error is to be found and leave it to the student to identify and correct the mistake.

Marking also needs to be positive as well as negative. Where students have done well in a particular aspect of the exercise, the fact should be commented on because we learn at least as much from our successes as from our failures.

The follow-up to marking is at least as important as the marking itself. It will not be practicable, nor in fact desirable, for every error to be corrected or the whole exercise re-worked until it is perfect. For example, it has already been pointed out in an earlier chapter that insistence upon correcting some kinds of typing error will achieve nothing for the student but, on the other hand, there are some like spellings or the misuse of words that must be corrected if the student is to learn. It is not possible to lay down hard and fast rules on this matter; much must depend on the judgement of the teacher, the nature of the error and the level of attainment of the students.

From time to time students can mark their own work from a perfect model (handout or OHP transparency) or the work of their fellow-students. In these instances, the assessment of the students' work should be on the accuracy and completeness of the checking.

Assessment

Assessment is an offshoot of marking, and here we are concerned with two methods. Firstly, we have to assess the work in relation to the work of the other students and this is commonly done by deciding upon a numerical or literal designation (10 or 20 marks or A, B, C, D, E) to give a ranking order for a whole class. Secondly, we have to assess the work according to the criteria that we have in mind at the particular stage of attainment reached—the standards that we are aiming at and that the student is well apprised of.

Most students will be seeking to qualify themselves by success in public examination and it is natural and desirable that they should do so. Consequently, teachers should always be very closely concerned with the syllabuses of the examinations that their students are aiming at, and indeed all the information that they can glean by one means or another (examiners' reports, examination bulletins, marking and assessment schemes, direct analysis of results arising from specific examinations) about the tests that their students will be attempting.

Unfortunately, teachers still face two important difficulties here. The first is that public examinations in the office skills are many and varied and, although they follow roughly similar lines, their differences are often as significant as their similarities. A score of different bodies conduct these examinations and there has so far not been enough rapprochement between them in order to establish standards. There is no guarantee, for example, that a student who passes an intermediate typewriting examination of the London Chamber of Commerce will pass the equivalent examination of the Union of Lancashire and Cheshire Institutes, or vice versa.

The second difficulty is that the public examining bodies have not hitherto disclosed their Pass or Fail standards or published for all to see their schemes of marking and assessment. Only Pitman Examination Institute has taken some steps along this road.

The jealous secrecy with which examining bodies shroud their schemes has never seemed wholly defensible; on the contrary, it has always seemed to the author that the examination loses absolutely nothing of its value if they are published for all to see and take note of. Grace McNicol said:

> The allocation of marks to most kinds of typewritten work seems to be very much a matter of individual judgement. There is no doubt, however, that the majority of teachers would welcome information from organized studies of desirable and practical standards to be expected from different types of students and courses, and about generally acceptable marking schemes. At present most schemes are evolved empirically and few, if any, are published. On the question of output employers do not seem able to give guidance on what might be a generally acceptable standard. The best one can do is to quote from the literature or other sources of knowledge which are available and to hope that this field of study will not remain neglected much longer. It cannot be stressed too often that the typewriting skill involves much more than copying a perfect original, and that the ability to use the manipulative skill intelligently, and with adaptability, is what is required at all levels of attainment not only at advanced levels.
>
> While typewriting is being marked the nature of the marking must change according to the goals aimed at. It may be convenient here to list these, allowing of course that the marking may often require the combination of these. In these cases, it is best if a distinction of colour is made, thus enabling both teacher and student to identify weakness and strength at a glance.

Typographical accuracy

Letters: Transposed, omitted, not fully struck, incorrect, raised or lowered, above typing line, crowded, piled, overtyped, shadowed.

Spaces: too few, in excess, incorrect.

Words: omitted, transposed, in excess, incorrect.

Margin: inconsistency in use.

Lines: out of alignment (squint), incorrect line spacing, wrong line-end divisions (best avoided).

Layout and display: wrong placement on paper, poor use of white space, inconsistent display method, faulty or inappropriate margins (including head and foot of paper), placement of headings and sub-headings, underscoring and/or ruling, legibility, intelligibility, line spacing (e.g. for money), relevance of layout to purpose, interpretation of instructions and action on them, quality of erasures and of carbons, correct conventions (e.g. in acronyms, dates, money), un-corrected errors, poorly corrected errors, output level against an expected standard.

Cognitive aspects

All those activities which involve thinking, planning, calculating, previewing, the exercise of judgement, initiative and decision. It is only recently that these indispensable activities have begun to receive the attention that is their due. The reader is referred to the work of Doris Holland, an account of some part of which appeared in the periodical *Office Skills* in January 1975.

It is good to be able to write that the Typewriting Examination Review Committee of the Royal Society of Arts has been considering very carefully and in detail the problems of assessment and marking of typewritten work. The Examinations Board of the Society was hoping to publish its full report in early 1976.

10 Curriculum, Course, Syllabus and Lesson

Curriculum means no more than 'course of study'; however, in modern educational practice it has come to have a rather more specialized meaning. The curriculum is usually taken to comprise all the educational activities of a school or college, or of the set of subjects of a course, and how they are related to one another, and how the necessary learning and instruction is organized for the whole institution or course. It can also mean the separate subject syllabuses combined together to constitute the curriculum for one particular group of students. We ought to recognize though that a set of subject syllabuses just thrown together does not in itself comprise a curriculum. Other considerations have to be taken into account if the curriculum is to be good and questions such as the following have to be raised and the best answers sought for the general purpose in mind:

What subjects are to be included? What subjects have the strongest claims for inclusion? What subjects are going to be excluded, and why? What are the demands of the different subjects it is decided to include, in terms of time allocation, level of importance, degree of intensiveness, equipment, books, teaching aids and accommodation needed for successful learning? How are the subjects included to be correlated? Is there in fact a case for correlation and will this make the overall learning more effective? Only too often it happens that when the solution to these questions are thought to be known, the practical circumstances, which in any case will need to be taken into account, turn out to require some different answers: the teachers are not available or, if they are, they have not the expertise or specialized ability to carry out this or that part of the curriculum desired; accommodation may not be available in the right place at the right time, and the same is true of equipment and books; or the decisions eventually taken on the curriculum may come within the authority of a person who has not sufficient knowledge of the separate items in it or of their special needs, with the result that a curriculum is eventually decided upon which is far less effective than it might be.

As an example of this problem, the demands of general (even academic) education on the one side, and those of vocational subjects on the other, are often never resolved in a way to satisfy either.

The creation of a curriculum in which the various and often strident demands of different subjects and theories are effectively met, together with a proper regard for all the local circumstances and resources in labour and materials, is always a difficult and sometimes a daunting task. Perfection is, by the nature of things, unattainable but thought, consideration and planning to achieve an acceptable balance is vital if teachers and learners are to work as efficiently and happily as they ought.

The point to remember is that a curriculum, whether for a school or a separate course, is more than the sum of the subject syllabuses. It must include considerations of balance, emphasis, correlation between different areas of the curriculum and co-operation between the teaching staff who operate it; it has to be framed with both the broad view of its total effectiveness and relevance, and the detailed view of how it is to work organizationally and administratively in mind.

In the field of our enquiry, specific courses with fairly clearly defined goals are the rule. These may be full-time, part-time (day release) or evening, and are given explanatory titles such as, to quote from the prospectuses of schools and colleges: One-year Secretarial Course, Secretarial Studies Extension Course, Shorthand-Typists' Course, Course for Medical Secretaries, Bi-lingual Secretarial Course, Clerk-Typists' Course, Personal Assistants' Course, and so on.

The course syllabus is therefore the starting point and will incorporate the examination syllabuses. It is rare that our examination syllabus by itself is either adequate or appropriate. There are, for example, some aspects of the work and conduct of a shorthand-typist that are difficult, if not impossible, to test in a public examination as at present constituted, yet make up a vital part in the training of a learner following such a course. One might quote the ability of the learner to listen, comprehend and act upon an aural communication, or speak with a reasonable fluency and social acceptability. Confining a syllabus to the requirements of a particular examination is to do a disservice to the students.

Out of the course syllabus will be evolved the separate subject syllabuses (discussed in previous chapters) and out of them the teacher's scheme of work. This scheme is the central thread which links all the lesson plans and on which they should be based. New knowledge and skill needs to be linked to that already known, and reiterated and consolidated by use. Lessons are not therefore individual items separate from each other, but rather links in a chain, connecting with the future as with the past. What happens in a lesson now is bound to affect what happens tomorrow or in some future lesson.

In our field of study, in which an objective measure of attainment is largely attainable, it is right and natural that examination qualifications should be aimed at. The course syllabus must therefore take account of these and incorporate them into the syllabus.

There are no generally accepted rules for drawing up a course syllabus by topics but all of the following items should find a place:

(1) Number, age and entry qualifications of the students who are to follow the course.

(2) A general description of the nature of the course and what it will include.

(3) A clear and realistic statement of the aims in view—the targets of attainment.

(4) A statement of the allocation of time overall and within separate short periods (day, week or month).

(5) A statement of the books, materials, equipment and aids that are to be used.

(6) A statement of the methods to be used to achieve the goals stated.

(7) A statement giving the teacher(s) concerned and their responsibilities.

(8) A statement of the student records to be maintained.

(9) A step-by-step chronological scheme in outline but giving a fairly comprehensive picture (with sufficient detail to enable anyone reading it to understand clearly what is going on, or to enable another teacher, if the necessity arises, to pick up the threads and carry on). This is the scheme of work. It should also incorporate a reference to any tests or examinations to be taken en route, and to any revision or recapitulation that will be required.

Such a scheme of work is valueless unless it is realistic and practical and it—indeed a syllabus as a whole—is not a document to be compiled for the benefit of Principals, Heads of Department and HM Inspectors—and then quietly ignored. Its value lies precisely in that it should be so composed as to be indispensable at every point of time during the course.

From the scheme of work derive the lesson plans that the teacher writes for her own and her students' benefit. No doubt experienced teachers can give good lessons without benefit of notes of any kind, but how long can they keep it up without the work degenerating into a diffuse succession of activities lacking cohesion and showing no on-going purpose or logical progression? The best teachers always make notes of their lessons whether they have taught for two or twenty years; the fact that they do is one of the reasons why they are the best teachers.

Ideally, of course, a lesson should have a rounded unity and com-pleteness in itself; although this is not always possible it should evince a clear beginning, a middle and a well-defined end. In our field of study, peaks of effort are demanded of the students if they are to make progress and in planning any lesson a teacher ought to have in mind exactly when and where these will be called for.

It has always seemed to the author that a 60-minute period is quite appropriate for students whose ages are usually in the 16–25 range. Less than 45 minutes is not usually enough to give the lesson the body it should have, or allow enough time for the necessary student activities to be sufficiently developed, but it is realized that this is not always possible in the secondary field. The only justification it seems for lessons of greater length than this is in typewriting or transcription at a late stage in the course when the students have acquired a considerable measure of skill and need to build up their stamina in order to meet the demands of office or examination.

The form in which lesson notes are written is wholly a matter for the individual teacher although there are some items that are indispensable. These are: (a) the designation of the class; (b) date, time, location, dura-tion of lesson; (c) a breakdown of how the time is to be used and allocated to each part of the work planned; (d) the subject matter; (e) what you—the teacher—will do; (f) what the students will do; (g) all book references, examples, material to be used etc.; (h) what aids are to be used and such items as chalkboard examples or plan, OHP transparencies, key questions to be asked; (i) any special methods to be used.

Once a lesson plan has been drawn up on these lines, the mere act of thinking about it and doing it will imprint a picture on the mind, and although the notes should certainly be taken into the classroom and referred to whenever necessary, it will be found that the lesson will proceed without very much need for reference to them. Not, at any rate, in a way which may cause the students to think: 'Hello! She doesn't real-ly know what she's doing and she's having to look to find out what comes next.'

When notes have to be referred to, however, do not try to be covert about it; refer to them naturally, quickly, but quite ostentatiously. Make sure you have the transitions from one unit of work to the next in mind. The rest will come easily with experience.

It is natural human optimism to expect to get through more than in fact is possible. The idea that if you tell the students once they will have learned it, never works out in practice. How much to include in a lesson will come from experience.

A lesson plan is not an essay about a particular lesson but just a set of schematic and logical notes and references. It has already been stated that lesson notes are naturally individual but the format that the author has found most useful in practice and has usually used is arranged thus:

1 Factual details (class, date, time, lesson duration, note of absentees, main aims)

Time (min)	Content	Own activity	Student activity	Points to note

Actual examples will help to show the process in action. In order that the scheme of the lesson should be clear, the plans on pages 160–9 are fuller in content than the author would generally deem necessary but, apart from that, they are in fact notes of actual lessons. Four examples are given—one for a shorthand lesson (New Era), one for a PitmanScript, one for a transcription lesson, and one for Pitman 2000.

A convenient way of keeping lesson plans is in a looseleaf file. If this method is adopted, then the facing page is left free for notes which are invaluable both from the personal and the student-record viewpoint. Not a lesson will pass without the need for a note, and their accumulation over the weeks and months will make the problems of continuous assessment and of future lesson planning easier. The 'notes' page will be called into use for a variety of purposes, the most important of which are:

(*a*) It is very rarely that any lesson goes exactly according to plan. Excluding interruptions and chance occurrences, it may turn out to be too long or too short, the expected progress may not be made, or a change of plan may be necessary; the notes should reflect any such occasions. Often the reasons why something intended has not worked out as expected will be apparent at the time, though they may be forgotten later, and therefore should be noted down.

(*b*) Methods that work well and those that do not, or techniques that need to be looked at again should be noted. It sometimes happens that from the give-and-take of the lesson itself new teaching practices will evolve.

(*c*) Particular strengths or weaknesses of individual students are noted, along with general observations about their ability, temperament and attitudes.

(*d*) All items that need to be referred back to—such as a student's failure to produce promised work, an undertaking to find out the answer to a particular question, an observation to be passed on about a student's health or welfare, items borrowed by students, typewriter details and so on should all be entered.

(*e*) Points of interest and use often arise from students' questions and discussion. This is the place to write them down.

In short, any detail that springs from or is connected with the conduct of the lesson itself needs to be recorded. Such work is not too time-consuming, and it will pay dividends in more effective teaching out of all proportion to the time and trouble taken. The author would recommend any teacher, new or mature, to adopt the idea.

The lesson plans created for one course through a whole year of work will seldom remain unchanged for the next course. No two groups ever display exactly the same characteristics, each developing a recognizable ethos of its own; nor do any two progress in the same way or at the same rate. A body of lesson plans full of references, examples, illustrations, material for re-use and schematic planning will have a permanent value as a storehouse for the future, but the plans can never be transferred with entire success just as they stand from a class this year to the parallel class next year.

Whether we are in our first or our thirty-first year of teaching, we as teachers can learn from our own lesson plans and notes. We may often succeed and yet be conscious that we could do a still better job. Sometimes even the most experienced of us may fail, and then the lesson plan that began as a plan for success may face us at the end of the lesson as an indictment. That is the time when by self-searching and self-criticism we find out—with the help of our notes—what really went wrong.

1 Notes for a Shorthand Lesson. Introduction to Circle S

Class...... Course....... No. of students. .26. . . Absentees. . . .3. . .(names)

Location. Room 12 Date. 4 October 1975 Duration of lesson. 55 minutes

Time (minutes)		Content	Description	Student Activity	Notes
4	a	Why something special for S. Plurals, verbs.	Use telephone directory, dictionary. cp with other letters. Write large: knows, seems, business.	Find out how often S sound (or Z) occurs in 50 words. Copy. Is it S or Z in shoes, loss, nice, these, names.	Aural identification of S-Z sound.
8	b	S to curves.	Teach basic rule.	Read P.31 New Course examples. Copy: these, knows, loss, names, months, lose, invoice, seem, Sunday, sell, selling, sum, similar, sign.	Vowels IN. Spell: lose, similar.
5	c	Penmanship.	Use this sentence. Write up on chalkboard: Why pay this sum when we can get the same sales items for less on Wednesday? (16) Score speeds.	Copy. Slow repeat 3 times. Rule line. 30-second trial twice.	Aim—exact similarity last line as first.

			class.		
				duals repeat 'outline each'.	
5	e	Copy.	1–4 Ex. 24. Demonstrate Circle S to notebook group (4 students).	Copy—all vowels IN.	Circle S in isolation. Therefore: is the, has the.
6	f	Short Forms.	Teach: his, those, several, this, is, thus, as, has.	Drill SF in 3 orders.	
8	g	Copied dictation.	5–9 Ex. 24.	Copy from dictation. Read together. Repeat alone.	Part own dictation. Part individual students.
3	h	Recap on S with curves.	Q and A.		Add Z only medially or finally.
2	i	Free dictation.	60 words of Ex. 25 at 30 wam (give some help with outlines en route).	Students answer. Students take a note.	Insist on precise expression. Indicate line changes, phrases. Give punctuation.
6	j	Checking.		Check from book. Correct errors in margin.	
3	k	Free dictation.	Repeat at 50 wam. What success? Collect in 5 notebooks. (Next group for check and marking.)	Read back.	

2 Notes for a PitmanScript Lesson

Class. . . . . .   Course. . . . . .   No. of students. . 28 . . .   Absentees. . 2 . . . .(names)

Location. . 42 . . .   Date. . 2 Feb. 76 . . .   Duration of lesson. . 60 min. . . . .

Time (minutes)	Content	Description	Student Activity	Notes
4	Skill Book 1 Facility Practice 12.	Facility drills.	Read all lines. Copy with 3 blank lines.	Leave for out-of-class work. Point out that some vowels may safely be omitted in line (b).
3	Dictation Passage 12.	Preparation.	Read from longhand one sentence each round class.	Comment on *principal*.
8	PitmanScript of Dictation Passage 12.	Preparation from PitmanScript.	Read from PitmanScript. Stop at end of each sentence. Make copy of PitmanScript. Leave 2 blank lines.	Introduce shorter form for: *members*.
10	PitmanScript of Dictation Passage 12.	Preparation from PitmanScript.	Copied dictation at 50 wam. Two 'takes' with a one-minute interval. Read back first 'take' only.	

5	pp. 60, 61.	Present the sounds of *k* and *kw*.	Copy, then read all examples. Use question and answer to check knowledge.	Use a simple table—beginning, middle, end.
12	p. 62.	Exercise 13.	Read with longhand. Re-read covering longhand. Copy into notebook leaving 2 blank lines.	Go directly to Exercise 13. Come back to special signs and links later. Keep class together on the initial copying by slow dictation, speed decided by observation of 4 or 5 students.
3	pp. 58, 59.	Present special signs and links.	Present on chalkboard or OHP without textbooks. Copy—read—dictate—re-read.	Different approach based on acquired knowledge during Exercise 13.
2½	p. 62.	Reprise of Exercise 13.	Copied dictation at 60 wam on second blank line.	Use *Handbook* and stopwatch. Break it into 2 'takes'.
4	p. 63.	'Unseen' preparation for Dictation Practice 9.	Ten words and links from Dictation Practice 9 written on chalkboard in longhand: she, office, magazine, official, she-will-be-able-to, although, and-I-think, likely, next-month, initially.	Check students' attempts. Write up correct forms. Students copy correct forms.

2 Notes for a PitmanScript Lesson (*contd.*)

Time (minutes)	Content	Description	Student Activity	Notes
3	Vocabulary Drill preceding Dictation Passage 12.	Vocabulary.	Read. Cover longhand. Re-read.	Point out shorter forms for: change, changeless, coalfield.
3*	Vocabulary Drill preceding Dictation Passage 12.	Vocabulary.	Copy. Read from own notes.	
5*	PitmanScript of Dictation Passage 12.	Preparation from PitmanScript.	Copied dictation at 70 wam. Two 'takes', one-minute interval. Read back second 'take' only.	
2	Dictation Passage 12.	'Free' dictation.	Recorded dictation from second part of passage beginning 'Mr Fell then went on . . .' at 70 wam.	Check the success of this at beginning of next period.

* May have to be omitted. Include if time allows.

3 Notes for a Transcription Lesson

Class...... Course...... No. of students 24 Absentees 2 (names)

Location Typing Room A Date 4 October 1975 Duration of lesson 60 minutes

Class level 80–100 wam in shorthand 35–45 wam in typewriting

Time (minutes)		Content	Description	Student Activity	Notes
3	a	Spelling.	Slow dictation 8 sentences containing: separate, accommodation, unconscious, eighth, benefited, acquaintance, disappearance, permissible.	Record shorthand note.	60 wam.
3	b	Reading and checking.	Write up words in capitals, in printed lower case and in writing.	Read back. Check words.	
3	c	Spelling.	Re-dictate sentences at 80 wam.	Type transcript of eight words only. Check. Record score.	Continue to 100 per cent success.
2	d	Preparation for transcript.	Read aloud passage of 240 words (given below).	Listen.	Emphasize sentence end by pauses.

For passage on which Transcription Lesson is based, see p. 170.

3 Notes for a Transcription Lesson (*contd.*)

Time (minutes)		Content	Teacher	Student Activity	Notes
5	e	Preparation for transcript.	Q and A on: UK, housework (solid), versus, *in toto*, colleagues (spelling), potential, segment, use of parentheses, creches, flexible, women's (apostrophe), fulfilment, available (spelling).	Answer questions. Make notes from OHP or chalkboard.	Common Latin tags in English.
3	f	Preparation for transcript.	Write up all unusual words and phrases in shorthand.	Copy and practise.	
7	g	Dictation.	Dictate at 60 wam.	Make shorthand note. Read back.	Where are full stops? How to represent the 3 figures.
6	h	Dictation.	Re-dictate at 80 wam.	Make shorthand note. 3-minute read through for correction and improvement. Use audio cassette.	How many paragraphs? Punctuation points.
5	i	Trap words.	Slow dictation (60 wam) of sentences containing: their, effect, principal, whose, site, reign, its, berth. Write up words.	Make note. Read back. Check words.	

2	j	Trap words.	Dictate separate set of sentences for same words 80 wam.	Make note.	
5	k	Transcription.	Watch transcription.	Transcribe trap-word sentences on typewriter.	1½-line spacing, 20 space margin. Correct all errors. Insert name top left. Use simplified block layout. Hand in when satisfied or at end of 14 minutes. Passage will be allotted transcription speed.
15	l	Transcription.	Return to note of passage. Give instructions and time for transcript (14 minutes).	Transcribe prepared shorthand note.	
			Collect in all work for checking, marking and speed assessment.		

4 Notes for a Pitman 2000 Shorthand Lesson

Class......   Course......   No. of Students......   Absentees......*(names)*

Location......   Date......   *Duration of lesson* 45 minutes

Time (minutes)		Content	Description	Student Activity	Notes
3	a	Present CH, J, SH, Stroke S.	Chalkboard or flipchart.	Practice strokes.	Show differences of intensity and in shape of curves.
3	b	All examples on p. 27.	Single words.	Read. Copy into notebook.	Pace the copying.
3	c	Same examples.	Present on chalkboard *without* vowels.	Close books. Copy chalkboard outlines. Insert vowels.	Check.
7	d	P. 28 material.	Repeat processes (*b*) and (*c*).		Watch curve shapes.
6	e	Short forms, new and revised.	New short forms, p. 28, then cyclic group from units 1–6 (*Dictation Practice*, Section 2).	Read, copy, practice in given order; Then from audio cassette (Unit 2 of *Dictation Practice*).	Have cassette ready at right starting point.

2	f	Phrases, p. 29.		Read, copy; re-read phrases from own note; Ask students to suggest one or two different ones from same elements.	Call attention to getting *second*, even *third*, element of phrase in right place.
10	g	R & W Practice, p. 30	Familiarity building by seeing, hearing, thinking, writing; Cover key first; Teacher—read whole Exercise.	Now with help of key, read and copy in own time; limit: 10 minutes.	Circulate; Check writing with individuals; Check that 'b r a i n i s s w i t c h e d o n'. (This to be 'free' dictation beginning at tomorrow's lesson.)
4	h	SF Practice *Workbook I*, pp. 12–16.	Cassette guided.	Pre-read at increasing rates before audio.	Check accuracy both in writing and reading.
7	i	'Easy' Dictation, p. 6 *Dictation Practice* (230 words).		Teacher reads whole; Students follow *Workbook*; Students read from *Workbook*; first line copy from audio.	Watch; Help individuals.

Passage for the transcription lesson

Married women in the office.

'Thirty-eight per cent of the people who work in the UK are women—and sixty-two per cent of those women are married. In this survey we set out to investigate how married women, working in offices, cope with their two lives of career and domesticity. We wanted to know why they chose to work, how they solve the practical problems of housework versus overtime, and what effects working has on their family relationship. In an earlier survey we carried out on health in the office, we established that women become more reliable, consistent employees as they get older. Even when they have young families and run busy homes, they have *in toto* less time off than their younger colleagues. With married women who do not work as the last remaining potential reserve for labour recruitment, employers must take more account in the future both of the potential and actual needs of this important segment of the population.

'The introduction of more state nursery schools (there are less than 500 at the present time), playgroups, creches provided by employers, and more flexible working hours, are facilities which many women's action groups are pressing to have improved. Many women with children complain that they are unable to seek the additional fulfilment of a job because these facilities are not available to them.'

(*Alfred Marks Survey*, January 1972)

11 Testing and Assessing Student Attainment

During most courses of study students are likely to encounter a good deal of testing and examination, some of it incidental and informal, some integrated and formal—even frighteningly so. This has been a fact of educational life for a long time now. Certainly tests and examinations are fully in evidence in the office-skills field today—nowhere more so.

Examinations in general

In recent years examinations have come under heavy fire from several quarters, the main arguments levelled against them, whether they are internal or external, being that they often prove to be unfair—different examiners arriving at markedly different conclusions about the same work—that they are selective and discriminating since they cannot test the whole syllabus, that they make no allowances for the student's circumstances since they take place at a set time in a given spot, that they omit assessment of many things that are just as important as those that they do assess, and that their accreditation value is much exaggerated. Nevertheless, tests and examinations survive and in the view of most people rightly so.

Fortunately, we have learned a great deal about examinations and tests in the last few decades and are in a much better position to create better examinations. Readers who wish to pursue the modern theory of testing and examination are recommended to read four books and in the order given here: *An Examination of Examinations*, Hartog and Rhodes (Macmillan); *Examinations—Pass or Failure*, Rust and Harris (Pitman); *Measuring Educational Achievement*, Ebel (Prentice-Hall) and *Objective Testing in Education and Training*, Rust (Pitman).

Tests and examinations survive and are steadily improved for the following reasons:

(*a*) They fulfil in what is held to be the fairest way the ranking in order of attainment of the learning group.

171

(*b*) They act as a very widely accepted warranty of attainment in reaching defined levels of knowledge and skill, and in obtaining employment or entry into further more advanced courses of study.

(*c*) Their requirements, if most carefully worked out, stated, accepted, and acted upon, give an orderly structure and a final goal to the course of study and they bring a necessary homogeneity and general acceptability to what might otherwise be so widely diversified and different as to make comparisons or judgements impossible.

(*d*) They set targets of attainment that have a wide, if not universal, agreement among educationists.

(*e*) They can be and often are motivating to both student and teacher alike.

Testing for grading and testing for learning

There are some kinds of tests from which the learners actually learn by virtue of doing them; this is certainly true of some forms of internal testing used in office skills. Generally, though, it is reasonable to state that while the student is being tested or examined she is not learning. Herein lies a danger: if you spend too much time weighing and measuring the body instead of feeding it, you may finish up with a skeleton. Tests or examinations ought not to be undertaken unless their need and purpose is definite and clear to both teacher and testee.

Tests and examinations also survive because they meet a natural human desire on the part of both learner and teacher to find out what has been achieved and where they stand. We have to remember that testing applies just as much to the teacher as to the taught. To measure your efficiency as a teacher by virtue of your students' examination successes may often be quite unfair, yet there is some point in it, and it cannot be entirely unjust.

Testing for grading is one thing; testing for learning is another. In a grading test (as, for example, a typewriting speed-assessment test or a Civil Service entry test) it is generally necessary for it to be of a formal kind, all the group tested being required to take the same tests at the same time, and for a thoroughly researched marking scheme to be applied. Testing for learning poses different aims: here the teacher seeks to find out what the problems of individuals are in grasping and applying ideas, in their ability to recall and their difficulties in the performance of a skill. The testing methods will vary and so will the content according to the needs and the current abilities of the students.

If we remind ourselves that an accepted principle of learning is that only a small proportion of what we read or hear or practice is retained unless there is meaningful repetition, continuous application and consolidation, it becomes clear that testing for learning is much more important than testing for grading since we are seeking to discover what is *not* being comprehended or learned. For the improvement of our teaching, this is even more essential than finding out what the students really know and can do.

Some pertinent remarks on the subject of the value of tests are made by Robert Ellis in his book *Educational Psychology* (D. van Nostrand Inc., 1951):

(1) Tests ... have a very important influence on the methods of study used by students. If a teacher announces that an essay test or a true-false test will be given over a given assignment, the class will tend to make the kind of preparation best suited for the particular test. (In general it may be said that the tests will be more valid and reliable if the teacher does announce in advance the nature of the test.)

(2) Tests provide an opportunity for student expression. Reaction is an important part of the complete learning process. Without tests, learning would tend to be too much a process of absorption. If we are to use knowledge, we must usually be able to recall it. Frequently a student thinks he knows a topic, but when he tries to recall it he realizes that his knowledge is inadequate. Knowledge is not satisfactory until expression in proper form is possible.

(3) Tests given after teaching and during the progress of the course are a most important basis for the location of errors resulting from learning. No teacher and no student is perfect. For this reason it becomes important to locate errors that still persist and make an attempt to correct them. Tests should be analysed for this purpose.

(4) Tests furnish a basis for marks and reports of progress.

(5) Tests ... supply an additional motive for studying. ... Students make better progress in learning when they have a knowledge of the progress they are making.

To which the author would add, '... and when they have a clear goal in view'. For a survey of various modern methods of testing (essay-type, completion, true-false, multiple choice, selection, etc.) the reader is referred to the books already mentioned.

Public examinations in the office skills

When we come to look at what is available in public examinations for the office skills, the most immediate impression is that of their number and diversity. Examining in shorthand, typewriting, audio-typing and transcription (though as far as the author knows this last is nowhere so referred to) we find the Royal Society of Arts, Pitman Examinations Institute, the London Chamber of Commerce, the fourteen Regional Boards of the Certificate of Secondary Education, the Union of Lancashire and Cheshire Institutes, the Civil Service (not external but covering many thousands of learners and improvers), the Yorkshire Council for Further Education, the Scottish Business Education Council, the Welsh Joint Education Committee, the East Midland Educational Union, the Northern Counties Technical Examinations Council, and the Union of Educational Institutes. It is natural to ask a few questions:

Q. Is there really a need for so many different examining bodies?
A. The answer is probably 'yes'. They all thrive and they all aim to provide for particular, and sometimes special regional and local, needs.

Q. Do they all examine the same subjects?
A. No, but there is a considerable amount of common ground. The majority have examinations that cover the field we have been discussing.

Q. Are their subject syllabuses the same?
A. No. Here again there is common ground, but both the syllabuses and the papers set on them very often reveal on study not only differences of content but differences of approach and emphasis that must affect the kind of teaching that is done in those schools and colleges that use their examinations.

Take, as an example, examinations in shorthand as a separate subject of study. Few examine in shorthand theory and writing style—which is a pity. The argument is that shorthand is only worth testing at the level of livelihood-earning and therefore the common type of examination is one in which a passage is dictated at a strictly-controlled set speed and then has to be transcribed by the student either in writing or on the typewriter within a defined time and, except at the lower speeds, only the transcript is scrutinized for assessment. However, it is worth noting that Pitman Examinations Institute still examines in theory and penmanship, and some bodies like the Royal Society of Arts retain examinations at 50 and 60 wam, which can hardly be regarded as more than a preparation for the shorthand-in-employment-use stage. Theoretical accuracy and excellence of shorthand style are important factors in building speed and in ensuring perfect transcription and they ought not to be ignored in examinations. How much is to be dictated and in how many separate pieces of a defined length varies, not only among different examining bodies but also at different stages of attainment in the examinations of a single body.

There are very few clear and fully objective rules laid down about the subject matter, format, vocabulary or internal consistency of the material set for tests; one has to learn by studying past papers what to expect. This is not to say, of course, that all these reputable examining bodies pay no attention to these matters. They often give their examiners instructions and set up moderating committees in order to enquire into these things, but it is still a frequent and certainly not entirely unjustifiable complaint among practising teachers that consistency in the level of ease or difficulty is not maintained. In fact, this is a charge not infrequently levelled at all examinations, including those for office skills other than shorthand.

The major difficulty (but it is not an insoluble one) is that office-skills work through the medium of language and therefore it is hard to be as objective as might be desired. Useful and practical suggestions about this matter may be found in *The Art of Readable Writing*, Flesch (Collier-Macmillan), and—from another tack—in *Improve your English Reading*, Hunter Diack (Four Square).

It has often seemed to the author that in a shorthand test on which a valuable qualification depends and in which a candidate may fail irretrievably in the first half-minute, a preliminary oral reading of the passage, already provided for by some examining bodies, should precede every set speed dictation. The more so when one takes into account the fact that in the realistic office situation, the writer is likely to have a good prior notion of the kind of content and vocabulary to expect and is primed to cope with it, and will certainly be familiar with the dictating voice and closer to the dictator than is general in an examination room.

Nor do the examining bodies pay much regard to the nature or the expertise of the actual dictation. Timing is, of course, carefully controlled, but it is quite possible for a candidate to be called upon to take dictation in the examination from a voice not previously heard, while others have the powerful advantage that they are perfectly familiar with the voice, the regional pronunciations and the dictation mannerisms of the dictator, having taken dozens of pieces from this source previously.

This is not the place to go into a full and detailed discussion of examinations in the office skills in all their aspects, but it is worth noting that very little use has been made so far of the aid of educational technology in producing completely standardized and fault-free dictation for examinations. In Southern Australia, shorthand examinations have been conducted for many years using L/P recordings fed into individual earpieces.

Assuming agreement with some or all of the points made, it is left to the reader to discover which of the examining bodies are least reprehensible in these respects.

Q. Are entry qualifications the same?
A. The short answer is 'Yes' because generally no specific qualifications are called for.

Q. What information do the examining bodies give about the manner in which they award their marks and finally arrive at an assessment of an examination?
A. A good question. It has been traditional for a long, long time to treat such information as top-secret: marking schemes, arrangements for moderation, for re-scrutinizing border-line cases, and for adjusting the levels at which 'Pass' or 'Distinction' or 'Not Pass' are awarded are all highly confidential matters. For a fuller treatment see the author's articles in *Office Skills* (Pitman).

However, the climate in this matter is changing. Pitman Examinations Institute, for example, publish in full the methods by which they arrive at a Typewriting Speed Assessment, and incorporate in detail what—and what not—is to be penalized. The Royal Society of Arts states the marks awarded to individual items, and also gives much guidance through its examiners' reports and its regular bulletins from which the intelligent reader may cull a good deal of information about the assessment policy.

It is still true, though, that since there is no open and general publication of all the details of assessment, the relative standards of different examination bodies cannot be arrived at.

Q. Do all these examining bodies have formal contact so as to work out national standards for office-skills examinations?
A. No.

On the whole important question of assessment and evaluation of a student's work, the reader is referred again to Dr Bonney Rust's book on *Objective Testing*.

Before leaving this short and general survey of examinations in office-skills subjects, some comments now follow on the separate subjects we have been considering.

(a) Typewriting

Typewriting speed is best assessed by plain line-by-line copy in which the student's only goal is to record exactly what she sees as quickly and accurately as she can. The passages, therefore, should be long enough for speeds up to 100 wam and should indicate the line-stroke totals, the cumulative stroke and word totals so that the student always knows the point she has reached. No corrections are to be made. The errors to be penalized are clearly defined: letters or words transposed, letters over-typed, letters or words omitted or in excess, incorrect letters typed, letters above or below the typing line, spaces omitted or in excess, unduly faint impressions, 'shadow' impressions (usually with upper-case letters), squint lines, unevenness in left-hand margins, crowding or piling of letters, omission of whole section (usually attributable to picking up at the wrong point a word that appears twice within a line or two and acts as a false cue).

The passages should be selected and/or edited or composed so as to cover the whole keyboard with instances of figure-work and all normal punctuation and additional signs. Their content should be clearly within the comprehension range of the students and in vocabulary free from uncommon or technical words and within a syllabic intensity of 1·5.

Speed is decided on the point reached at the conclusion of the typing, which may be of 5 or 10 minutes duration or, at higher levels, longer. Success or failure is decided upon an error-tolerance scale related to time and speed level reached. (For a suggested tolerance scale that works well and is in line with average attainment see Pitman Examinations Institute Rules and Regulations, 1976–7.)

Typewriting display and tabulation   The basic criteria for displayed and tabulated work in typewriting may be taken as:

    (i) the typographical accuracy;
    (ii) the ease of legibility. Can the content be readily grasped?
    (iii) judgement and intelligence used in setting out the material so that the relative importance of the matter is emphasized.

These criteria will involve margins, use of space, the setting on the page, centring (if that is required), line spacing in its relation to headings and prominent material, underscoring and/or letter spacing, balance of columns in columnar work, use of leader dots, sense shown of the limited manipulative and keyboard resources of the typewriter to achieve the desired effect, extent to which instructions have been carried out correctly, quality of erasures, typing touch (on manual machines), knowledge of accepted conventions, quality of carbon copies.

Typing production work   The criteria for judging production work (of which displays and tabulations are a specialized area) are usually taken to be:

    (i) extent to which the work is usable in a realistic situation—its mailability;

    (ii) the output in a given time or the time taken to produce the finished work. In assessment, output measurement is now generally accepted.

The criteria will involve typographical accuracy, quality of corrections, errors uncorrected, observance of conventions already taught, some agreed scale of measurement of output/time, placing on the page, judgement used in layout, observance of any special instructions (see also Chapter 9). Cognitive aspects must also be assessed.

(b) Shorthand

The accuracy, fluency and quality of shorthand outlines are not to be ignored, even though in most public examinations no reference, or only a token one, is made to the shorthand notes. During the course of instruction, including the period of speed development up to at least 100 wam, the following items should always come into student assessment: theory knowledge, reading ability, penmanship, command of short forms and, of course, the ability to record and read back or transcribe a passage given at a fixed speed.

    Chapter 6 on the teaching of shorthand will have given many indications of the criteria to be followed. Some suggestions about the kind of assessment tests that are valuable in these different areas of shorthand study are now given:

    (i) Theory knowledge. Individual words, testing specific points of theory, position writing, vowel insertion. The study of an *ad hoc* piece of accurate facsimile shorthand, followed by a slow dictation unseen of the passage and a check on accuracy. A series of short objective questions ('Why is the **R** in the word *tomorrow* upwards?').

    (ii) Reading ability. Assessment on the basis of 'how much can you read in a given time?' or 'how long does it take you to read these 50/100 words?' Oral reading is the best way of assessing. Transcription is a different requirement.

    (iii) Penmanship. Assessment on the basis of accuracy of outline, lightness of impression, distinction and uniformity of strokes (light, heavy, large, small, correctness of formation, correctness of length), phrasing, correct placing of essential vowels, fluency of writing, clarity of writing, size of outlines, spacing of outlines. Penmanship speed drills.

(iv) Command of short forms. Ability to record individual short forms at fixed speeds 50–80 wam, ability to read back from own notes instantaneously. Ability to record and read back sentences very largely composed of short forms. The concentration here must be on immediate response whether of writing or of reading.

(v) Speed tests. Formal tests requiring students to write or type back from their notes recorded at fixed speeds should be kept to a minimum. They take up much time which is better used to improve the students' knowledge and skill in shorthand writing and reading. Usually assessment should be on the basis of reading back orally a fixed number of words from a note. In testing for learning as opposed to testing for grading it is as important to assess the note as it is to assess the reading back.

(c) Audio-typing

The assessment of audio-typing ability cannot readily be separated from the assessment of transcription in general. The criteria will involve correct interpretation of the conventions included in the dictation, observance of any instructions given, time taken to produce the completed piece *or* output achieved in a given time.

(d) Transcription

It has already been made clear in Chapter 8 on Transcription that this is a complex skill made up of a number of sub-skills and special areas of knowledge and ability. During the instruction, therefore (as opposed to formal testing of the kind required by such examinations as Shorthand-Typing—Pitman Examinations Institute, or the Shorthand- and Audio-Typist's Certificates—Royal Society of Arts), we need to have close regard to the factors that affect the total transcription skill. These are:

(i) Speed of dictation. If this is close to the writer's speed limit, difficulty of transcription is increased.

(ii) Level of content. Words, structures, idioms that are not well known to the transcriber are sure to cause difficulty and errors.

(iii) The time lapse between writing a shorthand note or aural input of the passage to be transcribed from tape or cassette and the requirement of transcription. Retention is subject to rapid fading.

(iv) The pressure of time. Too high a demand will push the transcriber into errors which could have been avoided had more time been allowed.

(v) The length of the transcription required. A complete piece is always better transcribed if divided into two or three parts of equal length.

(vi) The conditions for transcription. What are the conditions for seeing or hearing the note (clear notes written in ink, high-fidelity cassettes, etc.)? Imperfections in machine (typewriter or dictation machine). Environmental conditions: light, heat, ventilation, noise, etc.

(vii) The form in which the transcript is required.

(viii) Reading habits of the transcriber. The importance of this element referred to in the chapter on typewriting is of equal importance in transcribing.

(ix) Ability to judge what is required in spacing and layout of the transcript.

(x) The temperament, attitude and mood of the transcriber. Factors of health and mental state. In transcribing, these matters are even more important than in other office skills, primarily because of the complexity of the skill required.

From these factors affecting transcription skill, two important matters emerge. The first is the obvious necessity to include transcription training in any office-skills course. The assumption that because a student can write shorthand, type and operate a dictation machine she can *ipso facto* produce usable documents without this specific training in the transcription skill, is demonstrably wrong.

The second is that during the instruction in transcription we must be careful to proceed in a series of carefully planned steps in which the various elements in the skill are introduced, as far as possible, only one at a time. The in-course assessment will necessarily have to follow this pattern. There are many steps between what might be a first assessment, viz.

A transcript of about 50 words in four sentences already read, seen and prepared, and requiring only minimal setting and manipulative arrangements;

to what might be the requirement at the end of such a course, viz.

Recording in shorthand two letters and a memorandum from previously unseen and unheard material and in total length 100, 150 and 100 words, and then transcribing them at a required transcription rate of 20 wam with a 3 per cent error tolerance.

Marking and correcting*

A conscientious and diligent student who completes a required piece of work and submits it for assessment has a right to expect that the teacher will conscientiously and diligently read it, mark it and assess it.

On the other hand, the output of work from office-skills students is such that if the teacher sets out to mark and correct everything, the task will very quickly become impossible.

This is a situation that confronts every teacher of office skills and we have therefore to consider what is to be done about it. It may be best to begin by trying to answer some of the basic questions: Is marking necessary? What are its purposes? How can these purposes be best fulfilled? What kind of marking should be adopted? What corrections should be made—and how? What records should be kept?

Marking and assessment records are certainly essential. Some of the reasons are self-evident, but it may nevertheless be helpful to summarize them:

(*a*) Marks provide the basic statistics for records of individual and class progress and attainment.

(*b*) They enable objective comparisons to be made between students and between classes.

(*c*) They enable rank order to be established.

(*d*) They are a useful prognosis for the achievement of students in public examinations.

(*e*) Marking, when well done and correctly followed up, is of value to the individual student in improving knowledge and skill, and to the teacher in revealing individual strengths and weaknesses.

(*f*) Marking is also a way of maintaining student effort and interest.

The work records based on regular marking:

(*a*) Enable the teacher to adjust the scheme of work and lesson plans in accordance with revealed needs.

---

* This section should be read in conjunction with Chapter 9.

(*b*) Provide the basis for reports generally required by school or college authorities.

(*c*) Provide a check that syllabus requirements are being met.

(*d*) Enable continuity to be maintained when staff changes become necessary.

Let us now consider more narrowly some of these purposes. No marking is worth doing that is not of value to the student; what the student gets out of the marking is just as important as what the teacher puts into it and to some extent will depend on this factor. Marking needs to be positive as well as negative; errors and weaknesses must, of course, be located and pointed out, but so too must the lessons to be learned from these by the student.

There are errors and weaknesses where correction is inappropriate, but there are many more where the student should be expected to make the necessary corrections and show these up as an essential part of the marking and assessment process. To quote a few examples of each type:

(*a*) If a student has transposed two letters on the typewriter or has omitted a word by inadvertence, there is no point in demanding a re-type.

(*b*) If, however, the student has made two spelling errors and mistyped **e** for **i**, then there is good reason why we should require the student to re-type the misspelled words correctly both in upper and lower case, and do a sentence exercise full of **e**'s and **i**'s to establish once again the right striking responses for these letters. (A marking code is given in Chapter 9.)

In the marking of shorthand, helpful comments should always be added as well as the indication of error.

Marking may be complete and detailed. In this case, it is wise to try to avoid covering the whole exercise with red or coloured inks. Indicate minor errors with a short underscore; only give important errors or weaknesses a fuller treatment. Personal and confidential comment should be given as often as opportunity allows in conversation with individual students. Questions arising from the marking of students' work should be answered as near to the time of the actual working of the exercise as possible. Similarly, the value of corrected work back on the student's desk within 24 hours is at least three times greater than when it is returned a week later.

Marking may also be for specifics only. For example, you may mark shorthand for penmanship only, requiring the students to make their own corrections for accuracy, or a transcript may be marked for typographical accuracy only or for spelling and punctuation only.

Whether marking is to be complete or limited to some specifics, it is important that the students are informed of this both when the work is collected and again when it is returned to them.

Some objective assessments may be done on the spot and are the most useful for the quick reinforcement of whatever teaching points have been made.

It is always essential to insist that the students study their corrected work, and they should be given a minute or two to do this with the opportunity to ask questions if there is anything that they do not understand. Similarly, it is essential to follow up: if corrections are required the notes sections of your loose-leaf Lesson Plan book should be used to jot down the necessary memo, and then the corrected work must be re-scrutinized. This ought always to be done, even if it means that less work is marked because of this need for re-scrutiny. If the students do not benefit from the marking and the assessment, then it may as well not have been undertaken.

Now we turn to consider how teachers may best cope with the burden of marking which may easily, unless steps are taken to rationalize it, become overwhelming. There are four basic ways in which the weight of marking may be reduced and yet be to the benefit of the students rather than to their disadvantage. A teacher submerged by marking is certainly likely to be less effective, both because the energy and enthusiasm that is a vital part of teaching, particularly in the office skills, is sapped by the task, and partly because the time that ought to be used for planning, for thought and for self-improvement is no longer available.

The basic ways are:

(*a*) Marking for specifics.

(*b*) Marking only a selection of all the work of some students over a particular period (a single lesson or day's work).

(*c*) Selecting only a part of what has been accomplished for a particular period, but marking that part for all the students in the group.

(*d*) Arranging and controlling self-marking and checking (or partnership marking and checking) wherever this is appropriate and will in fact be helpful to the students.

To the first of these we have already referred.

The second way is to ask for all the work produced by a small proportion of the students, e.g. 5 out of 25, and mark and assess this fully and conscientiously. This procedure is repeated at short intervals so that within, say, a fortnight, all the students of the class have been assessed in this way. The advantage of this periodic close scrutiny is not only that the overall amount of marking is reduced but that the assessment and its follow-up can take on a tutorial quality, with a closer understanding of student and student ability, and a closer personal relationship between teacher and student.

The third way is to ask the class at the end of a period of instruction to submit one item only (not announced in advance, of course) for general assessment. Quite often, whatever the skill in question, the students will have engaged in various activities, some of which will not have required actual visual output and which may be (like oral reading in shorthand) assessed on the spot, and probably three or four different items for which a written product was required. Then only one of these is collected and afterwards examined, marked and assessed fully, then returned and followed up.

The fourth way is to have the checking and assessment done by the students. This is not to be regarded as a way of getting out of a responsibility by requiring the students to undertake one's own work; rather it is a way of teaching them the paramount importance in their own present and future work of reading through, checking and correcting all their work. The methods of teaching students this checking skill have already been described in Chapter 8. Sometimes students may be called upon to check their own work, sometimes that of their friends and neighbours in the class. Two matters become important at once: the first is that only work that lends itself to this kind of objective checking should be chosen for using this way of marking; the second is that the checking itself must be checked if the method is to be successful. It is not always essential to scrutinize every checking by every individual student, but here again the selection of 4 or 5 students' work will suffice to keep everyone on their toes. Furthermore, it is a process that requires careful instruction and control by the teacher. The students must be conducted step by step through the process that they are to follow in assessing their own or a fellow-student's work. So important is this that sometimes marks should be awarded not on the work itself, but on the level of the checking and correcting shown.

All the discussion on marking given here relates to 'testing for learning'. The kind of marking and assessment described should be regarded as a constructive element in the total teaching programme from which the student will be led to learn. In summary, the lines to follow may be expressed as:

(a) Mark conscientiously and comprehensively.
(b) Be positive and constructive as well as negative.

(c) Insist upon proper corrections where these are appropriate.

(d) Teach students how to read and check their own work.

(e) Do not allow the checking of students' work to become so burdensome that it detracts from other elements of teaching.

(f) Keep conscientious records.

As to the kind of records to be kept, there is, of course, no prescription, unless a particular authority specifies them. The author's own preference is for well-designed cards that cater for all of the following needs:

(a) Age, date of birth, full names, address, telephone number of student.

(b) Next-of-kin and some family details.

(c) Date of entry. Name of course or courses followed.

(d) Date of leaving.

(e) Record of marks or gradings given with a short description of each piece of work assessed, with its date.

(f) Levels of skill attained at different stages.

(g) Internal and public examinations with their results.

(h) General observations: notes on temperament, attitude, general demeanour and background. Any incidents or events having a bearing on the student's progress and attainments.

(i) Attendance record in hours.

(j) Record of first employment.

(k) Teacher's comments on the student's work.

Naturally such a record card is a confidential document and should be kept private and secure. It is best if such records can be maintained on the basis of one card for the whole of the student's work in a particular course on the grounds of economy of effort and administrative centralization. This type of record has been kept by Pitman Colleges for very many years and its value has been proved repeatedly by references requested to the information contained on it by students of 30 or 40 years before.

12 Teaching Qualifications and Teacher Training

It is a matter of common observation that learning is very greatly influenced by the personal qualities and characteristics of the teacher. This is generally true of all subjects but even more emphatically so in the office skills. No doubt the earnest student-teacher may gain much from the formalized training provided by teacher-training colleges and colleges of education, yet all the training in theories of learning, psychology of education, methodology and the necessary formal aspects of a teacher's work will add up in the end to less than the native gifts of the 'born teacher'.

Let us put this in another way: carefully planned and diligently pursued courses of teacher training will undoubtedly benefit all intending teachers; so likewise will courses of in-service training for practising teachers. What they cannot do is to make a teacher out of a person who has not the inherent ability and aptitude. Even the finest teachers will benefit from good training; the worst will probably be no better than they would have been without it.

Let us consider now what the chief of these natural endowments may be.

Any teacher needs to be constitutionally strong and free from physical defects. People who have not attempted teaching a class of 20 or 30 young people can have no real idea of the amount of nervous energy and physical stamina that is demanded by a week's teaching of perhaps 20 or 25 hours. Vision and hearing both need to be acute, for when either of these senses is dulled the difficulties of teaching are greatly increased. A teacher stands permanently in need of the gift of tongues: for effective teaching, speech needs to be clear, resonant, audible at a distance, fluent and unhesitating, mellifluous even. The voice has to be an instrument on which one can play with effect; it must have a wide range in pitch and intensity, and its timbre must capture and hold attention. The gift of a naturally attractive voice and of easy speech of the kind described is incalculably valuable.

So too is a natural, warm, human sympathy. Unless a bond of understanding, mutual respect and purposeful co-operation is established between teacher and students, teaching will lose much of its effects and learning is sure to be less effective. In this teacher–student relationship, good humour and a stable, controlled personality will play a great part: if a teacher is a natural humorist and can spontaneously and without sarcasm create good humour in others, this is an added bonus.

Office skills, more than most subjects, call for enthusiasm and dedication on the part of the teacher. Single-minded and sincere enthusiasm will quickly brush off on the students, positive encouragement and a spirit of we-can-do-it-together will engender the right attitudes and the essential determination to succeed which is a part of the skills-learning process.

This essential enthusiasm has to be carried along on a tide of effort and work; there is never any time in an office-skills lesson for sitting back or even for thinking out the problems. All the necessary thinking and planning has to be done outside the class. During the instruction periods the teacher has to work with the students and for them, and become totally involved in all the activities while still maintaining the command and the overall plan and goals in mind.

It is even possible to overdo this involvement. We have to strike a balance all the time between the needs of the group and the needs of the individual. Neglect the first and some of the members of the group will lose heart or go astray through a lack of understanding or a weakness in technique; neglect the latter and the essential communal spirit of the group which does so much to sustain the students will not be generated.

A naturally-gifted teacher who is enthusiastic and who works hard and devotedly may still make the mistake of over-teaching. There is no doubt that in the office skills the students learn most from practice, provided that it is carefully prepared so that they know just what it is that has to be done, and why. Formal teaching is necessary, but the less of it we can make do with the better. It is certainly as important for the teacher to help the students to find out for themselves as it is to tell them and explain, however good that explanation is.

The next observation about the teacher's requirements to cope with the task may seem needless at first glance; regrettably, at this time, the facts speak differently. Every teacher of the office skills should be expert in both knowledge and ability in the skills taught. For example, every teacher should be capable of typing with reasonable speed (50 wam) and considerable accuracy, capable of writing perfectly correct shorthand with good style in penmanship in a notebook at 100 wam as a minimum, capable of writing on a chalkboard or a flipchart with the same speed and fluency as a model for the students to follow, capable of transcribing continuously and unhesitatingly in any required format from shorthand note or audio cassette, be in possession of a full and up-to-date knowledge of all aspects of these skills so that the problems of display, layout, placement, tabulation, shorthand rules, outlines and phrases and the reasons for them, the stages in development of transcription skill and so on, are all clear and intellectually organized. Command of subject is naturally vital if teaching and learning are to be completely effective. From this viewpoint, every office-skills teacher remains a learner and a student for the whole of her working life. Although we are never in the position of knowing it all or having every new and old technique at our control, to begin teaching with an inadequate subject command is to invite disaster.

It is important that the teacher should be able to demonstrate effectively, and not only to show the students how, but to be able to analyse and bring out the essential parts of that demonstration, and then to synthesize them once again into the total skill required at that particular stage of learning. One weakness of office-skills teaching is that effective demonstration as a teaching technique is too seldom used.

In this consideration of subject command, there is one aspect we have not yet touched upon and that is the teachers' own command of language, and their ability to understand and help solve the student's problems of linguistic inadequacy. E. Stones, in his valuable book, *Introduction to Educational Psychology,* Methuen (University Paperbacks) has a comment:

> Most teachers, coming as they do from a section of the population which is extremely sophisticated in the use of language, do not realize its immense complexity. Because of their education and probably because of their upbringing, teachers will be at home manipulating the complex abstract relationships which spring from language and will often find it difficult to make adequate contact with children who lack the body of concepts which teachers use automatically. Whether or not the teacher develops methods of helping students to overcome the problems of inadequate linguistic ability, it is most essential that he realize that the problem exists.

An academic attitude, sometimes to be observed, is that the teachers of office skills are mere mechanics and 'a lesser breed' in the educational world. So far as this attitude has any justification at all—and for the most part it is entirely false—it may derive from the intense concentration and dedication of skills teachers to their own field. Yet our subjects have contacts in all directions: if we are to be good skills teachers we need to be concerned in much wider fields of reference, particularly in everything that concerns the study of our language, in related subjects like economics and statistics, and in the rapidly expanding world of machines and educational technology. Above all we need actual experience of what is going on in the office world and in every business development that can affect the present and the future of our students.

In this book there has been room only for a short account of some of the most important aspects of teacher qualities and abilities with reference to skills teaching. To pursue the subject further, the reader is recommended to read *The Art of Teaching*, Gilbert Highet, in the Methuen University Paperbacks series, and *Teach Yourself to Teach* (EUP).

We turn now to consider the ways in which a teacher may become 'qualified' in the sense defined by the Department of Education and Science, with some brief account of the type of training that is given in the Colleges of Education leading to teacher qualification.

It is clearly very important that all intending teachers should understand what is meant by 'qualified' since those who are not so qualified may not be employed in schools and VI Form colleges in secondary education, except according to specific prescriptions laid down by the State. Generally speaking, a 'qualified' teacher is one who has successfully followed a recognized full- or part-time teacher-training course at a College of Education or educational institution. For more complete information the DES Circular 11/73 is relevant and needs to be studied in detail. It is also important to understand what is meant by 'qualified' status because teachers employed in secondary education who are not so qualified may very easily find that they are subject to restrictions of various kinds in matters of pay, security of employment, holidays, privileges and rights. These may vary from one area to another, but operate in all. Such teachers are designated as 'instructors'. Paragraph 28 of Circular 11/73 is relevant and is quoted here:

Some of the activities which have come to be regarded as an integral part of the school curriculum demand specialized skills. Qualified teachers possessing the necessary skills cannot always be available in sufficient numbers in such fields as the playing of musical instruments, office arts and skills and similar commercial techniques, sports, games and pastimes and technical subjects. . . . Regulation 18 of the Schools Regulations 1959 as amended therefore permits the employment of a person who is not a qualified teacher to give instruction in a specialized art or skill or a group of related arts or skills provided that no qualified teacher is available to give the necessary instruction. The instructor cannot be employed in a more general teaching capacity.

These same restrictions do not at present apply in Further Education.

There are, therefore, only three categories of teachers in secondary schools:

(*a*) Qualified teachers, or teachers accepted as having qualified status.

(*b*) Student teachers.

(*c*) Instructors.

All unqualified teachers of these subjects come into this third category, even though they may have acquired, say, the Teaching Certificates of the Royal Society of Arts or the Joint Examining Board Diplomas; it is reasonable to say that the DES approves them and encourages teachers to take them, but they still do not rank for qualification. Other teaching certificates of lesser importance are offered by the Faculty of Teachers in Commerce and the Incorporated Phonographic Society.

Instructors who wish to acquire qualified status have the following possible ways open to them of doing this:

(*a*) By following one of the 3-year training courses (which may sometimes be reduced to 2 years in special circumstances) offered by Departments of Education and by Colleges of Education. The current list of these is given below:

THE NORTH EAST LONDON POLYTECHNIC
DEPARTMENT OF EDUCATION
The Barking Precinct, Longbridge Road
Dagenham, Essex RM8 2AS

NEVILLE'S CROSS COLLEGE
Durham

CITY OF NEWCASTLE-UPON-TYNE
COLLEGE OF EDUCATION
Eastlands, 49 Elmfield Road
Gosforth
Newcastle-upon-Tyne NE3 4BB

PHILIPPA FAWCETT COLLEGE
94–100 Leigham Court Road
London SW16

REDLAND COLLEGE
Redland Hill
Bristol BS6 6UZ

ST MARY'S COLLEGE OF THE SACRED HEART
Fenham
Newcastle-upon-Tyne NE4 9YH

SOUTHLANDS COLLEGE OF EDUCATION
65 Wimbledon Parkside
London SW19

SUNDERLAND POLYTECHNIC
Sunderland
Co Durham SR1 3SD

SWANSEA COLLEGE OF EDUCATION
Townhill Road
Cockett
Swansea SA2 0UT

CAERLEON COLLEGE OF EDUCATION
Caerleon, Newport
Monmouthshire NP16 1XJ

CARTREFLE COLLEGE OF EDUCATION
Wrexham
Denbighshire

CREWE COLLEGE OF EDUCATION
Crewe Road
Crewe CW1 1DU

DUDLEY COLLEGE OF EDUCATION
Castle View
Dudley
Worcestershire

KINGSTON UPON HULL COLLEGE OF EDUCATION
Cottingham Road
Hull HU6 7RT

To these must be added the four Teacher Training Colleges (Technical)
whose primary purpose is to provide technical training to supply the
needs of such teachers in Further Education. These are:

GARNETT COLLEGE
Downshire House
London SW15 4HR

BOLTON COLLEGE OF EDUCATION (TECHNICAL)
Chadwick Street
Bolton BL2 1JW

HUDDERSFIELD COLLEGE OF EDUCATION (TECHNICAL)
Holly Bank Road
Huddersfield HD3 3BP

WOLVERHAMPTON TECHNICAL TEACHERS' COLLEGE
Compton Road West
Wolverhampton WV3 9DX

The entry qualifications for the Colleges of Education are a minimum of five GCE 'O' level passes, but more generally five 'O' and two 'A' level passes. The four technical teacher-training colleges run 1-year courses and also 4-term sandwich courses for those who already have a teaching appointment in FE. In addition, there are some 2-year extra-mural courses run by these colleges at technical institutions.

The future of the Colleges of Education is affected by the implementing of the White Paper on Teacher Training, but it is probable that the courses in Business Studies will continue along with 3-year B.Ed or BA degrees and with Diplomas in Higher Education.

(*b*) A second possible way of acquiring qualified status is through the shortened courses of training specially designed for instructors. One-year full-time courses now run at Crewe, Dudley and Caerleon Colleges, and there is a 2-year part-time course at Sunderland Polytechnic. Garnett College (Technical Teacher Training) is also accepting secondary-school teachers (if they are full-time) as well as FE teachers in their Sandwich Course run in conjunction with South Bank Polytechnic, London.

(*c*) The third way is by special entry through application by a local education authority. Paras 15 and 16 in Circular 11/73 refer to this. Such a means of entry to qualification requires the employing authority and not the teacher concerned to take the initiative, and a specific grant of qualified teacher status by the Secretary of State. The author has no information of any successful application under this provision.

Intending student teachers who have lived in the UK for three years preceding their course receive free tuition and are usually eligible for a maintenance grant which is dependent on income. At its maximum this covers board and lodging, personal expenses and the cost of necessary travel.

Two useful pamphlets which give further references and sources of information are *Teaching in Technical Colleges* and *Careers in*

Teaching and are obtainable from the Department of Education and Science, York Road, London SE1 7PH.

The situation so far described is that which applies in England and Wales. In Scotland and in Northern Ireland, the circumstances are different and intending teachers should write for particulars of teacher training in the business studies field to the colleges concerned; for information on conditions of entry, qualified teacher status, grants, salaries and conditions, courses of training offered and career prospects from The Scottish Education Department, St Andrew's House, Edinburgh or The Ministry of Education for Northern Ireland, Rathgael House, Balloo Road, Bangor, Co Down.

The main qualification required by part-time teachers of shorthand, typewriting and for office practice is the Teacher's Certificate (in each of these separate subjects) offered by the Royal Society of Arts; in fact, this well-known qualification is held by very many full-time qualified teachers as well. Many technical colleges run evening courses in preparation for these Certificates and a list of these is published each year in the September issue of *Office Skills*. In addition, excellent correspondence courses for the examinations are available from Pitman Correspondence College, Park Street, Croydon CR9 3NQ. Many intending teachers wisely combine a college course with a correspondence course in their studies for these examinations. All the information about the Royal Society of Arts Teacher's Certificates is to be obtained on application to The Secretary, Examinations Board, Royal Society of Arts, 18 Adam Street, London WC2N 6AJ.

The Joint Examining Board Diplomas (separate Diplomas in shorthand and typewriting are available) are examinations which correspond very closely to the RSA Certificates but are only for students living outside the UK where RSA teachers' examinations are not held. Particulars are to be obtained from The Secretary, Joint Examining Board, 39 Parker Street, London WC2B 5PB.

All teacher-training courses, whether full- or part-time, leading to qualifications to teach office skills and business studies, incorporate the study of educational psychology and the principles of learning and teaching; the application of these principles to particular subjects; the methods, techniques and activities to be used in the learning process; guided teaching practice and observation; and, more generally, a study of the educational system of the country and of the theories and philosophy of education. Subject content and skills expertise may or may not be a part of the course (although it is an essential part of the RSA and Joint Board examinations referred to above).

All teachers and intending teachers will find the two periodicals published by Pitman of the greatest help and value. *Memo* and *2000* appear monthly and are primarily intended for the student; in essence it is a supplementary and up-to-date textbook. *Office Skills* is a monthly publication exclusively addressed to the teacher of office skills and containing a key to the shorthand of *Memo* and *2000*, together with a continuous provision of information, articles on methods, techniques, and principles of interest and use to all concerned with business education.

The Service Department of Pitman continues, as it has done for many decades, to provide help, guidance, information, promotion and publicity in the form of teaching aids, pamphlets, seminars and conferences in all aspects of skills training, and an individual service to any teacher who makes an enquiry or asks for information or help. Its activities are not confined to the UK, but extend to the English-speaking world outside North America (which has its own parallel provision for service).

Readers of this book will need no persuasion that teaching the office skills requires, no less than the teaching of any other subjects, a high degree of knowledge, skill, imagination, resourcefulness, planning and study. It also demands a twofold enthusiasm for the subjects themselves and for teaching as a way of life. Teachers of office skills must be, for a substantial part of their work, as much coaches and mentors as teachers in the more conventional sense. They have to guide, enthuse and lead their students; they must cajole, encourage, hasten and help the whole learning group and each individual in it. It is better that persons, however well qualified, who find that they have less than total enthusiasm either for the subjects or for teaching should not enter into it or continue in it if they realize their unsuitability or lack of natural aptitude.

But for the teachers who have these enthusiasms and remain learners as well as teachers all their days, it can truthfully be said that there are few more absorbing, more challenging or more rewarding vocations and few that contribute more to the individual learner or to the nation as a whole.

Appendix Most Commonly Mis-spelled Words

Asterisks * indicate very high frequency words.
Derivative words causing spelling problems are listed with the base word.

absence*
absorb
  absorption
accessible
accidental
  accidentally
accommodate*
  accommodation*
achieved
acknowledge
acquainted*
acquiesce
  acquiescence
addresses*
aerial
aggravate
aggregate
agreeable
all right*
amateur
among*
analysis
  analyses
ancillary
Antarctic
anxiety

apparent
appearance*
appropriate
Arctic
argument
arrangement*
ascend
athletic
audio
automation
awful

bachelor
beginning*
believed*
benefited
beneficial
breathe
  breathing
budgeted
bureau(x)
  bureaucracy
business*

category
  categories

ceiling
centre
  centering
  centred
certain*
chaos
  chaotic
choice*
clothes
college
colleagues*
coming*
committee*
compatible
comparative
competent
  competence
completely*
connoisseur
conscientious
conscious
consistent
convenience
correspondent
  correspondence*
corroborate

courteous
courtesy
criticism
cursory

deceive
decision*
deficient
definite*
desirable
desperate
deterrent
disappeared
disappointed*
disastrous
discipline
discrepancy
dissatisfied
distributor
dossier

efficient
  efficiency
eighth
eliminated

195

embarrassed
  embarrassment
emphasize
enthusiasm
equipped
  equipment
erroneous
especially*
essential*
exaggerated
excellent*
exercise*
exigency
  exigencies
exhausted
expenses*
extremely*

familiar*
feasible
February
financial*
foreign
forty
friend*
fulfilled
  fulfilment

gauge
genius
government
grammar
grievance
guard*
  guardian

harassed
height*
heroes
honorary
horrendous

humour
  humorous
hungry
hurriedly
hypocrisy
hypothesis

immediately*
immigrate
incidentally
incipient
independent*
indispensable
influential
inoculate
  inoculation
install
  instalment*
intelligence
irrelevant
irreparable
irresistible

knowledge*

liaison
livelihood
lose
  losing*
lounge
lying*

maintenance*
manoeuvre
marriage
medicine
Mediterranean
miniature
minutes*
movable
murmur

necessary*
negotiate
  negotiable
niece
noticeable*

occasion
  occasional
  occasionally*
  occasioned
occur
  occurred
  occurrence*
omitted*
omission
onus
opinion*

parallel
  paralleled
parliament
pastime
penicillin
permanent
permissible
perseverance
physical
planning*
pleasant
possess
  possesses*
potential
preceding*
predecessor
preference
  preferred
preliminary
prestige
privilege*
procedure*
professional*
professor

pronunciation
proprietary
psychology

quiet*

really*
received
recognize
recommend*
referred
  reference*
relieved
repetition
replaceable

scarcely*
secretaries*
seize
sentence*
separate
  separately*
severely
shining
similar*
sincerely*
sociological
  (sociology)
sonic
statutory
subtlety
successful
  successfully*
summary
supersede
suppression
surprise
surprising*
synonym
synonymous

technical

technological

tendency

transfer

transferred*

transference

transient

twelfth

unconscious

underrate

undoubtedly*

unnecessary*

until*

usual

usually*

vaccinate

valuable*

video

view*

Wednesday*

weird

wield

withhold

woollen